24.50

Intertemporal Macroeconomics

Contributions to Economics

Michael Carlberg

Intertemporal Macroeconomics

Deficits, Unemployment, and Growth

With 99 Figures
and 30 Tables

Physica-Verlag
A Springer-Verlag Company

Series Editors

Werner A. Müller

Martina Bihn

Author

Prof. Dr. Michael Carlberg

Department of Economics

Federal University

Holstenhofweg 85

D-22043 Hamburg

Germany

A printing grant by Federal University, Hamburg, is gratefully acknowledged.

ISBN 3-7908-1096-7 Physica-Verlag Heidelberg New York

Cataloging-in-Publication Data applied for
Die Deutsche Bibliothek – CIP-Einheitsaufnahme
Carlberg, Michael: Intertemporal macroeconomics: deficits, unemployment, and growth
Michael Carlberg. – Heidelberg: Physica-Verl., 1998
   (Contributions to economics)
   ISBN 3-7908-1096-7

Softcover Design: Erich Kirchner, Heidelberg

SPIN 10667333   88/2202-5 4 3 2 1 0 – Printed on acid-free paper

Preface

This book is concerned with the long-run effects of budgetary and financial policy on aggregate demand and supply. Here the long run is characterized by the accumulation of public debt and foreign assets. This gives rise to a number of questions. Will the long-run equilibrium be stable? What does long-run instability imply? Is the long-run multiplier smaller than the short-run multiplier? Can the long-run multiplier become negative? This book takes a new approach to macroeconomic policy. It assumes a growing economy, as opposed to a stationary economy. And it assumes that the government fixes the deficit rate, as opposed to the tax rate. It is argued that economic growth is an important factor of long-run stability. Similarly, it is argued that a fixed deficit rate is an important factor of long-run stability.

Previous versions of some parts were presented at the Conference on Money, Banking and Insurance, at the Annual Congress of the European Economic Association, at the Symposium on Operations Research, at the Annual Conference of the Royal Economic Society, at the Jahrestagung des Vereins für Socialpolitik and at the Conference on Dynamic Disequilibrium Modelling. I have benefited from comments by Friedel Bolle, Giuseppe De Arcangelis, Giancarlo Gandolfo, Ulrich Geiger, Alfred Maußner, Jochen Michaelis, Wolfgang J. Mückl, M. J. M. Neumann, Daphni-Marina Papadopoulou, Franco Reither, Karlhans Sauernheimer, Michael Schmid, Paul Bernd Spahn, Hans-Werner Sinn, Torsten Tewes, G. F. T. Wolswijk and Jürgen Wolters. In addition, Michael Bräuninger, Michael Cyrus and Philipp Lichtenauer carefully discussed with me all parts of the manuscript. Last but not least, Doris Ehrich did the secretarial work as excellently as ever. I wish to thank all of them.

CONTENTS

CHAPTER II. FLEXIBLE EXCHANGE RATE   149

Introduction

The focus of this book is on aggregate demand and supply in a growing economy, featuring the dynamics of public debt, foreign assets and domestic capital. What will be the implications of various shocks and policy measures?

As a rule, we shall assume unemployment. As an exception, we shall also consider full employment. The growing economy is characterized by population growth and technical progress. This in turn gives rise to output growth and income growth. Against this background, we shall take the per head approach. The dynamics of public debt, foreign assets and domestic capital has it that a budget deficit adds to public debt, that a current account surplus adds to foreign assets, and that domestic investment adds to domestic capital. It proves useful to do the analysis within the framework of a growing economy.

We shall trace out the processes of adjustment induced by various shocks. These shocks can originate in consumption, savings, investment, exports or imports; in government purchases of goods and services, budget deficits or taxation; in money supply or the exchange rate; in money wages, the growth rate or the foreign interest rate.

As a response to a shock, the government (the monetary authority) can take policy measures so as to defend full employment. Here the reaction can be either instantaneous or delayed. Endogenous fiscal policy means for instance: The government continuously adjusts its purchases and the budget deficit so as to maintain full employment. Likewise, endogenous monetary policy means: The central bank continuously varies the quantity of money so as to keep up full employment. And endogenous exchange rate policy means: The government continuously adapts the exchange rate so as to safeguard full employment.

It will be helpful to consider different scenarios: The economy can be closed or open. Money wages are fixed, flexible or slow. The exchange rate is fixed or flexible. The government can fix either the deficit per head or the tax per head (for that matter, the government can fix either the deficit rate or the tax rate). Fiscal policy, monetary policy, and exchange rate policy are exogenous or endogenous. Foreign assets may be denominated in domestic currency or in foreign currency.

Additional topics are: wealth in consumption function, money finance of budget deficits (as opposed to debt finance), crowding out, imperfect capital mobility, slow fiscal policy. There will be simple models, basic models, as well as full models. Numerical examples and diagrams serve to illustrate the main points.

The present monograph consists of two major parts. Part I deals with the closed economy, and part II with the open economy. Part I in turn is composed of three sections. The government fixes the deficit per head (section 1), the tax per head (section 2) or the tax rate (section 3). Properly speaking, part II addresses a small open economy with perfect capital mobility. Part II in turn is made up of two chapters. In chapter I the exchange rate is fixed, and in chapter II it is flexible. Each chapter divides into two sections, the economy without public sector, and the economy with public sector (public debt).

Now the exposition will be laid out in greater detail. Let us begin with the closed economy in part I. The government fixes the deficit per head, fiscal policy being exogenous (section 1.1.). When the government fixes the deficit per head, then, according to the budget identity, it must adjust the tax per head. The analysis will be performed within the setting of an IS growth model. Labour supply, expressed in efficiency units, grows at a constant rate.

First have a look at the public sector. The government raises loans and levies a tax in order to finance its purchases of goods and services as well as the interest payments on public debt. The government fixes its purchases in per capita terms. Here per capita signifies per head of labour supply. Then multiplication by labour supply gives government purchases. In the same way, the government fixes its deficit in per capita terms, so multiplication by labour supply gives the budget deficit. The budget deficit, in turn, adds to public debt.

Next catch a glimpse of the goods market. Disposable income can be defined as factor income plus public interest minus taxes. Households consume a fixed share of their disposable income. Firms fix investment in per capita terms. Investment per head times labour supply equals investment. Output is determined by aggregate demand, the goods market clears.

The long-run equilibrium is characterized by the condition that public debt per head does not move any more. This raises a number of questions. Will the long-run equilibrium be stable? Take for instance an increase in government purchases and the budget deficit per head. In the short run, this brings up output per head. Then, in the medium run, public debt per head accumulates. What will be the dynamic effects on output per head?

In section 1.3., we proceed to endogenous fiscal policy. As a response to a shock, the government continuously adjusts its purchases per head and the budget deficit per head so as to maintain full employment all the time. Can this be sustained? Consider a fall investment per head. In the short run, to counteract this, the government raises its purchases per head and the budget deficit per head. That is why, in the medium run, public debt per head goes up. How should fiscal policy answer to this?

In section 2.1., the government fixes the tax per head, fiscal policy being exogenous. When the government fixes the tax per head, then, according to the budget identity, it must adjust the budget deficit per head. In the long-run equilibrium, the motion of public debt per head comes to a halt. Will the long-run equilibrium be stable? Regard an increase in government purchases per head, holding the tax per head constant. In the short run, this lifts output per head. And in the medium run, public debt per head starts to grow. How does this impinge on output per head?

In section 2.2., fiscal policy becomes endogenous. That is to say, the government continuously varies its purchases per head so as to always keep up full employment. Is this feasible in the long run? Imagine a cut in investment per head. In the short run, to prevent unemployment, the government steps up its purchases per head. Therefore, in the medium run, public debt per head builds up. How should fiscal policy react to this? In full analogy, in section 3, we study the economic consequences of a fixed tax rate.

At this juncture, we leave the closed economy (part I) and enter the open economy (part II). For the time being, let the exchange rate be fixed (chapter I).

First consider the basic model of an economy without public sector (section 1.1.). We take a small open economy with perfect capital mobility. For the small open economy, the foreign interest rate is given exogenously. Under perfect capital mobility, the domestic interest rate agrees with the foreign interest rate. Therefore the domestic interest rate is constant, too.

To begin with, have a look at the foreign sector. Exports are fixed in per capita terms. Exports per head times labour supply yields exports. Domestic residents hold foreign assets and earn interest on them. The income of domestic residents includes domestic income and the interest inflow. Imports are a certain fraction of the income of domestic residents. Exports plus the interest inflow minus imports constitute the current account surplus. The current account surplus in turn adds to foreign assets. Next we are concerned with the goods market. Domestic residents consume a fixed share of their income. And domestic output corresponds to the demand for domestic goods.

The long-run equilibrium is characterized by the invariance of foreign assets per head. Will the long-run equilibrium be stable? Regard for instance an increase in exports per head. In the short run, this drives up output per head. Then, in the medium run, foreign assets per head accumulate. How does this affect output per head? Second suppose a rise in investment per head. In the short run, this boosts output per head. Because of this, in the medium run, foreign assets per head start to decline. How does this feed back upon output per head?

In section 1.6., exchange rate policy becomes endogenous. Put differently, the government continuously adjusts the exchange rate so as to defend full employment all the time. Can this be sustained? Think of a drop in investment per head. In the short run, the government must devalue domestic currency. For that reason, in the medium run, foreign assets per head pile up. What does this imply for exchange rate policy?

In section 2.1., we introduce the public sector, fiscal policy being exogenous for the moment. The government fixes its purchases and the budget deficit, in per capita terms, respectively. The budget deficit contributes to the accumulation of public debt. The government makes interest payments on public debt. The disposable income of domestic residents is the sum of factor income, interest inflow and public interest, diminished by taxes. Imports are a certain fraction of the disposable income of domestic residents. Exports plus interest inflow minus imports gives the current account surplus. The current account surplus in turn contributes to the accumulation of foreign assets.

In the long-run equilibrium, public debt per head and foreign assets per head stop to adjust. Will the long-run equilibrium be stable? Suppose that the government increases its purchases and the budget deficit per head. In the short run, this raises output per head. In the medium run, public debt per head starts to grow, while foreign assets per head start to decline. What will be the effect on output per head?

In section 2.3., fiscal policy becomes endogenous. The government continuously adjusts both its purchases per head and the budget deficit per head so as to safeguard full employment all the time. Is this feasible in the long run? Consider a cut in exports per head. In the short run, the government augments its purchases and the budget deficit per head. On those grounds, in the medium run, public debt per head begins to accumulate, whereas foreign assets per head begin to decumulate. Which fiscal policy is needed to absorb these side effects?

At this stage, we move on from fixed exchange rates (chapter I) to flexible exchange rates (chapter II). First consider the basic model of an economy without public sector. Essentially we follow the same lines as before. Exports per head are an increasing function of the exchange rate. Now catch a glimpse of the money market. Money demand is an increasing function of the income of domestic residents. The central bank fixes the money supply in per capita terms. In equilibrium, money demand equals money supply.

The long-run equilibrium is characterized by foreign assets per head being constant. Will the long-run equilibrium be stable? Regard for instance an expansion of money supply per head. In the short run, this measure brings up output per head. That is why, in the medium run, foreign assets per head are heaped up. How does this influence output per head? Next imagine a rise in investment per head. In the short run, output per head does not respond. Later on, in the medium run, foreign assets per head begin the fall. Again, what are the consequences for output per head?

Another section is devoted to endogenous monetary policy. The central bank continuously adapts the money supply per head so as to maintain full employment all the time. Can this be sustained? Let there be a reduction in investment per head. In the short run, the central bank need not intervene. Then, in the medium run, foreign assets per head pile up. How should the central bank answer to this?

Finally, in section 2, we install the public sector, fiscal policy being exogenous. In the long-run equilibrium, public debt per head and foreign assets per head do not change any more. Will the long-run equilibrium be stable? Suppose the government increases its purchases and the budget deficit per head. In the short run, output per head remains unchanged. As time goes on, in the medium run, public debt per head starts to grow, while foreign assets per head start to decline. What does this mean for output per head?

Brief Survey of the Literature

This book deals with the dynamics of public debt and foreign assets. Accordingly the present survey aims at the dynamics of public debt and foreign assets, too. Giving a rough outline, we shall proceed in three steps. To begin with, we shall consider a closed economy, featuring the dynamics of public debt. Then we shall come to an open economy without public sector, featuring the dynamics of foreign assets. At last we shall arrive at an open economy with public sector, featuring the dynamics of both public debt and foreign assets.

1) Closed economy, dynamics of public debt. The existing literature represents four strands of thought: the isolated dynamics of public debt, the supply-side effects of public debt, the demand-side effects of public debt, and the interaction between supply and demand. Let us start with the isolated dynamics of public debt. The basic reference is the paper by Domar (1944). There are neither supply-side nor demand-side effects of public debt. The underlying notion is that a budget deficit contributes to the accumulation of public debt. Therefore the government has to make higher interest payments. This in turn increases the budget deficit, thereby speeding up the accumulation of public debt. The government can follow either of two strategies, it can fix the deficit rate or the tax rate. If the government fixes the deficit rate, then, according to the budget constraint, the tax rate becomes endogenous. On the other hand, if the government fixes the tax rate, then the deficit rate becomes endogenous.

As a result, stability depends on the choice of strategy as well as on the rate of income growth. First assume a fixed deficit rate. In a growing economy, the long-run equilibrium will be stable. In a stationary economy, however, the long-run equilibrium will be unstable. Ultimately, public debt will tend to explode. Second assume a fixed tax rate. In a growing economy, there is a stability condition. If the interest rate exceeds the growth rate, the long-run equilibrium will be unstable. The other way round, if the interest rate falls short of the growth rate, the long-run equilibrium will be stable. From the empirical point of view, the interest rate exceeds the growth rate, so the long-run equilibrium will be unstable. In a stationary economy, of course, the long-run equilibrium will always be unstable.

We come now to the supply-side effects of public debt. There is full employment, and the economy operates at the capacity constraint. The investigation is conducted within the framework of neoclassical growth theory. The seminal papers are by Diamond (1965) as well as by Phelps and Shell (1969). The basic idea is that budget deficits crowd out private investment, thus reducing the stock of capital and hence aggregate supply. More exactly, an increase in the deficit rate reduces capital per head and output per head. It lowers consumption per head, provided the interest rate surpasses the growth rate.

First suppose a fixed deficit rate. In a growing economy, the long-run equilibrium will be stable. But in a stationary economy, the long-run equilibrium will be unstable. Public debt will tend to explode, thereby driving the stock of capital down to zero. Second suppose a fixed tax rate. In a growing economy, there is a stability condition. If the interest rate is higher than the growth rate, the long-run equilibrium will be unstable. Conversely, if the interest rate is lower than the growth rate, the long-run equilibrium will be stable. Empirically speaking, the interest rate is higher than the growth rate, so the long-run equilibrium will be unstable. It goes without saying that, in a stationary economy, the long-run equilibrium will be unstable. Neither the isolated dynamics of public debt nor the supply-side effects of public debt will be treated here. For a modern approach to these subjects see e.g. Carlberg (1995).

The next point refers to the demand-side effects of public debt. The economy suffers from both unemployment and excess capacity. The analysis is carried out within the setting of Keynesian theory. The basic idea is that the government must make interest payments on public debt to the private sector. This in turn raises disposable income, consumption and thus aggregate demand.

The main results of the present monograph can be summarized as follows. First consider a fixed deficit rate. In a growing economy, the long-run equilibrium will be stable. In a stationary economy, however, the long-run equilibrium will be unstable. Eventually public debt and output become very large. Second consider a fixed tax rate. In a growing economy, there is a stability condition that empirically is open to question. In a stationary economy, of course, the long-run equilibrium will always be unstable.

In the existing body of literature it is generally assumed that the government fixes the tax rate and that the economy is stationary. On those grounds, the long-run equilibrium will be unstable. Further, introducing wealth into the consumption function leads to a stability condition that empirically is uncertain. The key reference here is the paper by Blinder and Solow (1973). They study the long-run consequences of fiscal policy within an IS-LM model. A rise in government purchases causes a rise in output, where the long-run effect goes beyond the short-run effect. They obtain a stability condition that empirically is open to question. Infante and Stein (1976) argue forcibly that, in Blinder and Solow (1973), either the long-run equilibrium is unstable, or the long-run multiplier is negative. Christ (1978, 1979) augments the Blinder-Solow model by a Phillips curve. He reaches the conclusion that the long-run equilibrium will be unstable. Possen (1979) seems to be the only one who allows for economic growth. He postulates a fixed tax rate and finds out a stability condition. Scarth (1979), Cohen and de Leeuw (1980) as well as Smith (1982) proceed to endogenous fiscal policy. In Scarth the long-run equilibrium is unstable. In Cohen and de Leeuw as well as in Smith there is a stability condition.

2) Open economy, dynamics of foreign assets. The literature takes four avenues: the isolated dynamics of foreign assets, the supply-side effects of foreign assets, the demand-side effects of foreign assets, both effects simultaneously.

Let us begin with the isolated dynamics of foreign assets. The basic reference is the paper by Domar (1950). There are neither supply-side nor demand-side effects of foreign assets. The underlying notion is that a current account surplus contributes to the accumulation of foreign assets. Therefore domestic residents earn more interest on foreign assets. This in turn raises the current account surplus, thereby speeding up the accumulation of foreign assets. Exports per head are constant. The income of domestic residents consists of domestic income and the interest inflow. Imports are a given proportion of the income of domestic residents. In a growing economy, there exists a stability condition that empirically is doubtful. And in a stationary economy, the long-run equilibrium will always be unstable. As time goes on, foreign assets grow without limits (or, for that matter, foreign debt grows without limits).

We address now the supply-side effects of foreign assets. The labour market clears, and capacity is fully utilized. The analysis is performed within the framework of neoclassical growth theory. Important papers are by Hamada (1966) and Buiter (1981). The basic idea is that savings increase net exports. More precisely, a lift in the saving rate induces a lift in foreign assets per head. Consumption per head improves, so long as the interest rate is greater than the growth rate. In a growing economy, there is a stability condition that empirically seems to be sound. In a stationary economy, on the other hand, the long-run equilibrium will be unstable. Both foreign assets and consumption tend to explode. Neither the isolated dynamics of foreign assets nor the supply-side effects of foreign assets will be dealt with here. For a modern approach see e.g. Carlberg (1997).

Finally have a look at the demand-side effects of foreign assets. There is unemployment, and the economy operates below capacity. The investigation is conducted within the setting of Keynesian theory. The basic idea is that domestic residents hold foreign assets and earn interest on them. The interest inflow pushes up the income of domestic residents, their consumption and thus aggregate demand.

The main results of the present monograph can be summed up in the following way. First regard a fixed exchange rate. In a growing economy, there is a stability condition. From the empirical point of view, this condition is likely to be met. In a stationary economy, however, the long-run equilibrium will be unstable. Ultimately, both foreign assets and output become very large. Second imagine a flexible exchange rate. In a growing economy, the long-run equilibrium will be stable. Conversely, in a stationary economy, the long-run equilibrium will be unstable. Foreign assets grow without limits, which brings output down to zero.

The existing body of literature generally assumes a stationary economy. For that reason, the long-run equilibrium will be unstable. Further, putting wealth into the consumption function gives rise to a stability condition that, empirically speaking, is open to question. The paper by Buiter (1978) rests on a Mundell-Fleming model with perfect capital mobility. The exchange rate is flexible, and agents hold exchange rate expectations. Prices are slow, and agents hold inflation expectations. He posits a growing economy, which is a rare exception. Moreover he takes money finance of budget deficits for granted. Emphasis is laid on the oil price shock. He does not do any stability analysis, because the model is rather complex. The paper by Rodriguez (1979), too, is based on a Mundell-Fleming model with perfect capital mobility and a flexible exchange rate. Contrary to

Buiter, he starts from a stationary economy with fixed prices and ends up with a stability condition. The treatise by Allen and Kenen (1980) centers around a portfolio that is made up of domestic money, domestic bonds and foreign bonds. The exchange rate is either flexible or fixed. Also they get a stability condition. The paper by Branson and Buiter (1983) is concerned with a flexible exchange rate and reaches a stability condition.

3) Open economy, dynamics of public debt and foreign assets. The literature divides into two lines of reasoning: The supply-side effects of public debt and foreign assets, as contrasted with the demand-side effects of public debt and foreign assets. We set out with the supply-side effects. There are no idle resources. The analysis is performed within the framework of neoclassical growth theory. The underlying notion is that budget deficits crowd out net exports. More exactly, an increase in the deficit rate reduces foreign assets per head. Consumption per head deteriorates, provided the interest rate exceeds the growth rate.

First consider a fixed deficit rate. In a growing economy, there is a stability condition that empirically seems to be sound. Yet in a stationary economy, the long-run equilibrium will be unstable. Both public debt and foreign debt tend to explode. Second consider a fixed tax rate. In a growing economy, there is a stability condition. If the interest rate is higher than the growth rate, the long-run equilibrium will be unstable. The other way round, if the interest rate is lower than the growth rate, the long-run equilibrium will be stable. In a stationary economy, needless to say, the long-run equilibrium will be unstable. The supply-side effects of public debt and foreign assets will not be discussed here. For a modern approach, see e.g. Carlberg (1995).

We conclude with the demand-side effects of public debt and foreign assets. The economy suffers from unemployment, and there is excess capacity. The investigation is carried out within the setting of Keynesian theory.

The main results of the present monograph can be summarized as follows. Suppose that the government fixes the deficit rate. First take a fixed exchange rate. In a growing economy, there is a stability condition that, empirically speaking, will be fulfilled. And in a stationary economy, the long-run equilibrium will be unstable. Second take a flexible exchange rate. In a growing economy, the long-run equilibrium will be stable. But in a stationary economy, the long-run equilibrium will be unstable.

The existing body of literature relies on the premise that the government fixes the tax rate, and that the economy is stationary. As a consequence, the long-run equilibrium will be unstable. Then, inserting wealth into the consumption function leads to a stability condition that empirically is uncertain. The papers by Scarth (1975, 1977) and Katz (1977) build on a Mundell-Fleming model with perfect capital mobility. The exchange rate can be flexible or fixed. The long-run equilibrium proves to be unstable. In the paper by Turnovsky (1976) foreign bonds are imperfect substitutes for domestic bonds. The exchange rate is fixed. He derives a stability condition. In the paper by Allen (1977) as well as the treatise by Allen and Kenen (1980), the exchange rate is either flexible or fixed. The long-run equilibrium turns out to be unstable.

Turnovsky (1979) proceeds to endogenous policy. Strictly speaking, he evaluates a mix of monetary and fiscal policy. The exchange rate can be flexible or fixed. He obtains a stability condition. Klausinger (1986) examines both exogenous and endogenous policy. Under a fixed exchange rate, in any case, the long-run equilibrium will be unstable. Under a flexible exchange rate, stability depends on the type of policy. If policy is exogenous, the long-run equilibrium will be unstable. If policy is endogenous, there is a stability condition. The treatise by Frenkel and Razin (1987, 1992, 1996) rests on exogenous policy. The long-run equilibrium is demonstrated to be stable, which comes as a surprise. This can be attributed to a very large effect of wealth on consumption. Under a fixed exchange rate, the long-run effect of fiscal policy is even greater than the short-run effect. And under a flexible exchange rate, fiscal policy is ineffective.

Simple Models of a Stationary Economy

1. Closed Economy

1.1. Fixed Tax Rate

Let us begin with the public sector. The government levies a tax and raises loans in order to finance its purchases of goods and services as well as the interest payments on public debt. Properly speaking, the government fixes its purchases of goods and services $G = \text{const}$. The government pays the interest rate $r = \text{const}$ on public debt D, so public interest amounts to rD. The government imposes a proportionate tax T on factor income Y and public interest $T = t(Y + rD)$ with tax rate $t = \text{const}$. The budget deficit can be defined as the excess of government purchases and public interest over tax revenue $B = G + rD - T$. The budget deficit in turn adds to public debt $\dot{D} = B$. Here the dot denotes the time derivative $\dot{D} = \partial D / \partial u$ with time u. From this one can deduce $\dot{D} = G + rD - t(Y + rD)$.

Next have a look at the goods market. Disposable income Y_d consists of factor income Y and public interest rD, net after tax respectively $Y_d = (1 - t)(Y + rD)$. Households consume a given fraction of disposable income $C = cY_d$ with consumption rate $c = \text{const}$. Firms fix investment $I = \text{const}$. In the short-run equilibrium, output equals aggregate demand $Y = C + I + G$. This implies $Y = c(1 - t)(Y + rD) + I + G$.

Accordingly the short-run equilibrium can be represented by a system of two equations:

$$Y = c(1-t)(Y+rD)+I+G \tag{1}$$
$$\dot{D} = G+rD-t(Y+rD) \tag{2}$$

Endogenous are $\dot{D}$ and Y. Now solve (1) for output (income):

$$Y = \frac{I + G + c(1-t)rD}{1 - c(1-t)} \tag{3}$$

An increase in government purchases causes an increase in output (and employment). The same applies to an increase in public debt. Further eliminate Y in (2) by means of (3) to get:

$$\dot{D} = \frac{(1-c)(1-t)(G+rD) - tI}{1 - c(1-t)} \tag{4}$$

Then differentiate (4) for D to arrive at:

$$\frac{\partial \dot{D}}{\partial D} = \frac{(1-c)(1-t)r}{1 - c(1-t)} > 0 \tag{5}$$

As a result, the long-run equilibrium will be unstable.

At last we shall keep track of the process of adjustment generated by an increase in government purchases. Initially the economy is in a long-run equilibrium without public debt. The budget is balanced, and output does not change. Against this background, the government raises its purchases. In the short run, as a response, output goes up. The budget moves into deficit. In the medium run, the budget deficit contributes to the accumulation of public debt. The government has to make more and more interest payments to the private sector. This enhances disposable income, consumption and hence output. In addition, the rise in public interest augments the budget deficit, thus speeding up the accumulation of public debt. In the long run, both public debt and output tend to explode. It will be argued that, in a growing economy, the long-run equilibrium will be stable (see part I, section 3).

1.2. Fixed Budget Deficit

We start right out with the public sector. The government fixes its purchases of goods and services G = const. Likewise the government fixes the budget deficit B = const. The budget deficit in turn adds to public debt $\dot{D} = B$. Government purchases plus public interest minus the budget deficit gives the required level of taxation $T = G + rD - B$.

We come now to the goods market. Disposable income is the sum of factor income and public interest, diminished by taxation $Y_d = Y + rD - T$. Take account of $T = G + rD - B$ to verify $Y_d = Y + B - G$. Households spend a certain fraction of disposable income on consumption $C = cY_d$ with c = const. Firms fix investment I = const. In the short-run equilibrium, output corresponds to aggregate demand $Y = C + I + G$. From this follows $Y = c(Y + B - G) + I + G$.

The short-run equilibrium can be written as a system of three equations:

$$Y = c(Y + B - G) + I + G \tag{1}$$

$$\dot{D} = B \tag{2}$$

$$T = G + rD - B \tag{3}$$

Here $\dot{D}$, T and Y are endogenous. Next solve (1) for output:

$$Y = \frac{I + G + c(B - G)}{1 - c} \tag{4}$$

Suppose that the government increases its purchases and the budget deficit, by the same amount respectively $\Delta B = \Delta G$. Judging by (4), this measure brings up output. An increase in public debt, however, has no effect on output. Beyond that differentiate (2) for D to find:

$$\frac{\partial \dot{D}}{\partial D} = 0 \tag{5}$$

As a consequence, the long-run equilibrium will be unstable.

To illustrate this, we shall trace out the process of adjustment induced by a fiscal expansion. At the beginning, the economy is in a long-run equilibrium without public debt. The budget balances, and output is invariant. In this situation, the government raises its purchases and the budget deficit. In the short run, this action lifts output. The budget gets into deficit. In the medium run, the budget deficit gives rise to the growth of public debt. Output, on the other hand, does not react. The growth of public debt is accompanied by the growth of public interest. In order to cover this, the government must raise taxation. In the long run, public debt and tax revenue grow without limits. But output stays fixed, apart from its short-run jump. It will be argued that, in a growing economy, the long-run equilibrium will be stable (cf. part I, section 1). Figures 1 and 2 show the time paths of public debt and output.

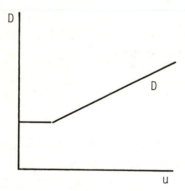

Figure 1
Time Path of Public Debt
(Fixed Budget Deficit)

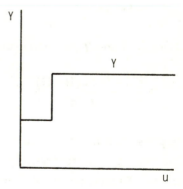

Figure 2
Time Path of Output
(Fixed Budget Deficit)

2. Open Economy

2.1. Fixed Exchange Rate

The analysis will be performed within a small open economy characterized by perfect capital mobility. For the small open economy, the foreign interest rate is given exogenously $r^* = $ const. Under perfect capital mobility, the domestic interest rate coincides with the foreign interest rate $r = r^*$. Thus the domestic interest rate is constant, too.

Let us start with the foreign sector. Exports are assumed to be fixed $X = $ const. Domestic residents earn the interest rate r on foreign assets F, so the interest inflow amounts to rF. The income of domestic residents consists of domestic income and the interest inflow $Y + rF$. Imports are a fixed share of the income of domestic residents $Q = q(Y + rF)$ with import rate $q = $ const. The current account surplus is identical to exports plus interest inflow minus imports $Z = X + rF - Q$. The current account surplus in turn adds to foreign assets $\dot{F} = Z$. This yields $\dot{F} = X + rF - q(Y + rF)$.

Besides, a few words will be said on the goods market. Domestic residents consume a certain fraction of their income $C = c(Y + rF)$ with $c = $ const. Let $q <$ c. Firms fix investment $I = $ const. Domestic output agrees with the demand for domestic goods $Y = C + I + X - Q$. From this one can derive $Y = (c - q)(Y + rF) + I + X$.

The short-run equilibrium can be described by a system of two equations:

$$Y = (c - q)(Y + rF) + I + X \tag{1}$$

$$\dot{F} = X + rF - q(Y + rF) \tag{2}$$

Endogenous are $\dot{F}$ and Y. Solve (1) for output:

$$Y = \frac{I + X + (c - q)rF}{1 - c + q} \tag{3}$$

An increase in exports leads to an increase in domestic output, as can be learnt from (3). The same holds for an increase in foreign assets. Moreover get rid of Y in (2) with the help of (3) and rearrange:

$$\dot{F} = \frac{(1-c)(X+rF) - qI}{1-c+q} \qquad (4)$$

Then differentiate (4) for F to ascertain:

$$\frac{\partial \dot{F}}{\partial F} = \frac{(1-c)r}{1-c+q} > 0 \qquad (5)$$

Put another way, the long-run equilibrium will be unstable.

To see this more clearly, catch a glimpse of the process of adjustment set in motion by an export shock. At the beginning the economy is in a long-run equilibrium without foreign assets. The current account is balanced, and output is uniform. In these circumstances, exports go up. In the short run, as a response, output also comes up. The current account registers a surplus. In the medium run, due to the current account surplus, foreign assets pile up. The ensuing swell in the interest inflow boosts the income of domestic residents, their consumption and hence output. Over and above that, the swell in the interest inflow enhances the current account surplus, thereby accelerating the piling up of foreign assets. In the long run, foreign assets and output become very large. It will be argued that, in a growing economy, the long-run equilibrium will be stable (cf. part II, chapter I).

2.2. Flexible Exchange Rate

Let us begin with the foreign sector. Exports are an increasing function of the exchange rate $X = je$ with sensitivity $j = const$. Here e symbolizes the exchange rate. Domestic residents earn the interest rate r on foreign assets F, so the interest inflow is rF. Foreign assets are denominated in domestic currency. The income of domestic residents is composed of domestic income and the interest inflow $Y + rF$. Imports are a given proportion of the income of domestic residents $Q = q(Y + rF)$ with $q = const$. The current account surplus can be defined as exports augmented by the interest inflow and diminished by imports $Z = X + rF - Q$. The current account surplus in turn adds to foreign assets $\dot{F} = Z$. From this one can conclude $\dot{F} = je + rF - q(Y + rF)$.

Next we shed some light on the goods market. Domestic residents consume a certain fraction of their income $C = c(Y + rF)$ with $c = const$. Firms fix investment $I = const$. Domestic output equals the demand for domestic goods $Y = C + I + X - Q$. This yields $Y = (c - q)(Y + rF) + I + je$.

Then we address the money market. Money demand is an increasing function of the income of domestic residents $L = \kappa(Y + rF)$ with sensitivity $\kappa = const$. Without losing generality, let $\kappa = 1$. The central bank fixes the money supply $M = const$. In the short-run equilibrium, money supply is in harmony with money demand $M = L$. Taking all pieces together, we get $M = Y + rF$.

The short-run equilibrium can be captured by a system of three equations:

$$Y = (c - q)(Y + rF) + I + je \tag{1}$$

$$M = Y + rF \tag{2}$$

$$\dot{F} = je + rF - q(Y + rF) \tag{3}$$

Here e, $\dot{F}$ and Y are endogenous. Solve (2) for domestic output:

$$Y = M - rF \tag{4}$$

An increase in money supply raises output. An increase in foreign assets, on the other hand, lowers output. Further have a look at the exchange rate. Solve (1) for $je = (1 - c + q)(Y + rF) - I - rF$ and throw out $Y + rF$ by means of (2):

$$je = (1 - c + q)M - I - rF \tag{5}$$

An increase in money supply bids up the exchange rate, which amounts to a depreciation of domestic currency. An increase in foreign assets, however, cuts back the exchange rate (appreciation). Moreover eliminate je in (3) with the help of (1) and reshuffle terms $\dot{F} = (1 - c)(Y + rF) - I$. Now pay attention to (2):

$$\dot{F} = (1 - c)M - I \tag{6}$$

Then differentiate (6) for F to find out:

$$\frac{\partial \dot{F}}{\partial F} = 0 \tag{7}$$

As a consequence, the long-run equilibrium will be unstable.

Coming to an end, we keep track of the process of adjustment kicked off by a monetary expansion. Initially the economy is in a long-run equilibrium without foreign assets. The current account is balanced, and output does not move. Against this background, the central bank increases the money supply. In the short run, this measure depreciates domestic currency, thus stimulating exports. That is why output goes up. The current account experiences a surplus. In the medium run, the current account surplus contributes to the accumulation of foreign assets. The increase in foreign assets, in turn, appreciates domestic currency, thereby curbing exports and hence output. And the rise in the interest inflow enlarges the current account surplus, which speeds up the accumulation of foreign assets. In the long run, foreign assets tend to explode. Therefore output comes down to zero. Eventually the economy must collapse. It will be argued that, in a growing economy, the long-run equilibrium will be stable (see part II, chapter II).

PART I

CLOSED ECONOMY

1. Fixed Deficit Per Head

1.1. Exogenous Fiscal Policy

When the government fixes the deficit per head then, according to the budget identity, it must adjust the tax per head. The investigation will be carried out within an IS growth model. N denotes labour supply, expressed in efficiency units. n symbolizes the growth rate of labour supply (in efficiency units), which by assumption is constant. The growth rate includes the rate of population growth and the rate of technical progress. It holds $\dot{N} = nN$. Here the dot stands for the time derivative $\dot{N} = \partial N / \partial u$ with time u.

First have a look at the public sector. The government raises loans and levies a tax in order to finance its purchases of goods and services as well as the interest payments on public debt. Strictly speaking, the government fixes its purchases of goods and services in per capita terms $g =$ const. Here per capita means per head of labour supply (in efficiency units). Then multiplying government purchases per head by labour supply gives government purchases $G = gN$. Likewise the government fixes its deficit in capita terms $b =$ const. Then multiplying the budget deficit per head by labour supply gives the budget deficit $B = bN$. The budget deficit in turn adds to public debt $\dot{D} = B$. Similarly the government fixes the tax in per capita terms $t =$ const. Then multiplying the tax per head by labour supply gives tax revenue $T = tN$. The government pays the interest rate $r =$ const on public debt D, so public interest amounts to rD. The government budget identity has it that the excess of government purchases and public interest over the budget deficit must be covered by tax proceeds $T = G + rD - B$. This can be restated as follows $tN = gN + rD - bN$. Here b, g, r, D and N are exogenous, while t is endogenous.

Next consider the goods market. Disposable income can be defined as factor income and public interest, net after tax respectively $Y_d = Y + rD - T$. Households fix the marginal consumption rate $c =$ const. Without loss of generality, let there be no autonomous consumption. Therefore the consumption function is $C = cY_d$. Now substitute $T = G + rD - B$ into $Y_d = Y + rD - T$ to obtain $Y_d = Y + B - G$. Then take account $B = bN$ and $G = gN$ to get

$Y_d = Y + bN - gN$. Further put this into the consumption function $C = c(Y + bN - gN)$. Firms fix investment on a per capita basis $i = $ const. Then multiplying investment per head by labour supply gives investment $I = iN$. In the short-run equilibrium, output agrees with aggregate demand $Y = C + I + G$. Assembling all component parts, we arrive at $Y = c(Y + bN - gN) + iN + gN$.

On this foundation, the short-run equilibrium can be represented by a system of four equations:

$$Y = c(Y + bN - gN) + iN + gN \tag{1}$$

$$\dot{D} = bN \tag{2}$$

$$tN = gN + rD - bN \tag{3}$$

$$\dot{N} = nN \tag{4}$$

Endogenous are t, $\dot{D}$, $\dot{N}$ and Y.

It proves useful to do the analysis in per capita terms. Income per head is defined as $y = Y/N$. Accordingly equation (1) can be formulated in per capita terms $y = c(y + b - g) + i + g$. Public debt per head is defined as $d = D/N$. Take the time derivative of public debt per head $\dot{d} = \dot{D}/N - D\dot{N}/N^2$. Observe $\dot{D} = bN$ and $\dot{N} = nN$ to arrive at $\dot{d} = b - nd$. Equation (3) can be written in per capita terms as $t = g + rd - b$. The short-run equilibrium in per capita terms can be characterized by a system of three equations:

$$y = c(y + b - g) + i + g \tag{5}$$

$$\dot{d} = b - nd \tag{6}$$

$$t = g + rd - b \tag{7}$$

Here $\dot{d}$, t and y are endogenous.

What are the chief properties of the short-run equilibrium? To answer this question, solve equation (5) for output per head:

$$y = \frac{i + g + c(b - g)}{1 - c} \tag{8}$$

Judging by equation (8), an increase in investment per head causes an increase in output per head. The same applies to an increase in government purchases per head (or, for that matter, in the budget deficit per head). An increase in public debt per head, however, has no effect on output per head. The same is true of an increase in the growth rate.

Now we shall go into some details. First regard an increase in investment per head. The short-run multipliers are $\Delta y = \Delta i / (1-c)$ and $\Delta t = 0$. Of course, this is due to the fact that we have a lumpsum tax. Second imagine an increase in government purchases and the budget deficit per head. More precisely, assume that the government raises its purchases and the budget deficit by the same amount, in per capita terms respectively $\Delta b = \Delta g$. The short-run multipliers are $\Delta y = \Delta g / (1-c)$ and $\Delta t = 0$. Output per head rises, whereas the tax per head remains unchanged. Third suppose that the government increases the budget deficit per head, holding its purchases per head constant. The short-run multipliers are $\Delta y = c\Delta b / (1-c)$ and $\Delta t = -\Delta b$. That is to say, the government reduces the tax per head, thereby bringing up consumption per head and output per head. Fourth take an increase in government purchases per head, keeping the budget deficit per head constant. The short-run multipliers are $\Delta y = \Delta g$ and $\Delta t = \Delta g$. In other words, the government raises its purchases and the tax by the same amount, in per capita terms respectively. In this instance, too, the balanced budget multiplier is unity.

At this point we leave the short-run equilibrium and come to the long-run equilibrium. In the steady state, public debt per head does not move any more $\dot d = 0$. Thus the long-run equilibrium can be captured by a system of three equations:

$$y = c(y+b-g)+i+g \tag{9}$$

$$nd = b \tag{10}$$

$$t = g+rd-b \tag{11}$$

The endogenous variables are d, t and y.

What are the salient features of the steady state? Solve (9) for output per head:

$$y = \frac{i + g + c(b - g)}{1 - c} \tag{12}$$

As a fundamental result, the long-run equilibrium of output per head is identical to its short-run equilibrium, cf. equation (8).

In addition, (10) provides public debt per head:

$$d = \frac{b}{n} \tag{13}$$

Let the growth rate be positive $n > 0$, since otherwise there would not exist a steady state. In a stationary economy $n = 0$, for example, there is no long-run equilibrium. Obviously, an increase in the budget deficit per head raises public debt per head. An increase in the growth rate, on the other hand, lowers public debt per head.

Besides, substitute $d = b/n$ into $t = g + rd - b$ to check:

$$t = g + br / n - b \tag{14}$$

Let the interest rate exceed the growth rate $r > n$, which from the empirical point of view seems to be sound. It is evident that an increase in government purchases per head leads to an increase in the tax per head. The same holds for an increase in the budget deficit per head. But an increase in the growth rate leads to a reduction in the tax per head. Now assume that the government increases both its purchases per head and the budget deficit per head $\Delta b = \Delta g$. Then the long-run multiplier will be $\Delta t = (r / n)\Delta g$. As a consequence, the government must increase the tax per head by more than its purchases per head $\Delta t > \Delta g$.

Next we shall probe into stability. Differentiate equation (6) for d to verify:

$$\frac{\partial \dot{d}}{\partial d} = -n \tag{15}$$

Here two cases can occur. In a growing economy (n > 0), the long-run equilibrium will be stable. In a stationary economy (n = 0), however, the long-run equilibrium will be unstable. Henceforth, let be n > 0.

To illustrate this, we shall trace out the process of adjustment induced by a fiscal expansion. Initially the economy is in the long-run equilibrium. Government purchases per head and the budget deficit per head are invariant. The same applies to public debt per head, the tax per head, output per head and consumption per head. The economy suffers from unemployment. In this situation, the government lifts its purchases and the budget deficit by the same amount, in per capita terms respectively $\Delta b = \Delta g$. In the short run, this policy measure enhances output per head, thereby alleviating unemploment. The tax per head does not respond, and consumption per head improves.

In the medium run, the lift of the budget deficit per head contributes to the accumulation of public debt per head. On that account, the government must make more interest payments per head to the private sector. In order to finance this, the government must lift the tax load per head. In spite of that, disposable income per head does not move. Clearly, two counteracting forces are at work. The rise in public interest per head pushes up disposable income per head, and the rise in the tax per head pulls down disposable income per head. Because the rise in the tax per head equals the rise in public interest per head, the net effect on disposable income per head is zero. That is why consumption per head and output per head do not move either.

As time goes on, the economy approaches a new long-run equilibrium. Finally public debt per head, the tax per head, and output per head stop changing. To sum up, there is a one-time jump in output per head and consumption per head. Public debt per head and the tax per head grow asymptotically. In this sense, a fixed deficit per head can be sustained.

Figures 1 until 4 show the associated time paths. Figure 1 displays the autonomous paths of government purchases and the budget deficit, in per capita terms respectively. Here u stands for time. Figure 2 reveals the induced path of output per head. Likewise figure 3 exhibits the asymptotic growth of public debt per head. Figure 4 graphs the exogenous path of government purchases per head and the endogenous path of the tax per head. In the short run, there is a one-time

28

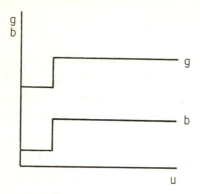

Figure 1
Government Purchases and
Budget Deficit Per Head

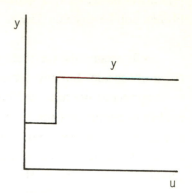

Figure 2
Output Per Head

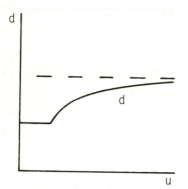

Figure 3
Public Debt Per Head

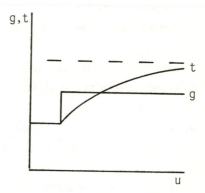

Figure 4
Government Purchases
and Tax Per Head

jump in government purchases per head. In the medium run, the tax per head rises well above government purchases per head. And what is more, the time path of consumption per head is equivalent to that of output per head, cf. figure 1.

So far we assumed a lumpsum tax. Now, instead, we shall consider a proportionate tax. Strictly speaking, the government levies a tax at the flat rate $t = const$ on factor income and public interest $T = t(Y + rD)$. Then the budget identity in per capita terms is $t(y + rd) = g + rd - b$, where t is endogenous. This substitution has no effect on output per head or public debt per head, the only difference being in the tax rate itself.

Finally we shall give a short summary. In a growing economy, the long-run equilibrium will be stable. In a stationary economy, on the other hand, the long-run equilibrium will be unstable. Regard for instance an increase in government purchases and the budget deficit per head. In the short run, this action drives up output per head. Then, in the medium run, public debt per head and the tax per head start climbing. Output per head, however, does not move any more. Put another way, there is a one-time jump in output per head. In this sense, exogenous fiscal policy can be sustained. For the basic idea of this model and further applications see Carlberg (1996).

1.2. Numerical Example

To illustrate this, take a numerical example with $c = 0.9$, $i = 8$, $g = 20$, $b = 0$, $n = 0.02$ and $r = 0.04$. At the beginning, let the economy be in the long-run equilibrium. According to equation (12) from section 1.1. output per head is $y = 100$. The budget is balanced $b = 0$, so there exists no public debt $d = b/n = 0$. Equation (14) yields the tax per head $t = 20$, which of course equals government purchases per head $g = 20$. The consumption function $cc = c(y + b - g)$ has it that consumption per head is $cc = 72$.

Against this background, the government increases its purchases per head from 20 to 21 and its deficit per head from 0 to 1. In the short run, this measure brings up output per head from 100 to 110. In the medium run, public debt per head starts to accumulate, rising continuously from 0 to 50. In spite of that, output per head stays at 110. In other words, the short-run multiplier is 10, and what is more, the long-run multiplier is the same size. In the short run, the tax per head remains unchanged. In the medium run, it climbs from 20 to 22. In the short run, consumption per head improves from 72 to 81. In the medium run, it stays at the higher level. In the short run, the sum of consumption and government purchases, in per capita terms respectively, goes up from 92 to 102. In the medium run, this sum is uniform. In the medium run, public interest per head swells from 0 to 2. And the debt-income ratio is pushed up from $d/y = 0$ to 0.45.

Table 1 presents a synopsis of this process. Column 1 gives the long-run equilibrium before shock, column 2 the short-run equilibrium after shock, and column 3 the long-run equilibrium after shock.

Table 1
Closed Economy
Increase in Government Purchases and Budget Deficit Per Head

	1	2	3
g	20	21	21
b	0	1	1
y	100	110	110
d	0	0	50
t	20	20	22
rd	0	0	2
cc	72	81	81
cc+g	92	102	102

Next consider an increase in the budget deficit per head from 0 to 1, holding government purchases per head constant at 20. Initially let the economy be in the steady state. In the short term, the fiscal expansion drives up output per head from 100 to 109. In the intermediate term, public debt per head comes into existence, growing slowly from 0 to 50. Nevertheless output per head stays at 109. The short-term multiplier is 9, as is the long-term multiplier. In the short term, the government lowers the tax per head from 20 to 19. In the intermediate term, it raises the tax per head up to 21. In the short term, consumption per head is lifted from 72 to 81. In the intermediate term, it does not move any longer. For an overview, see table 2.

Table 2
Closed Economy
Increase in Budget Deficit Per Head

	1	2	3
b	0	1	1
y	100	109	109
d	0	0	50
t	20	19	21
cc	72	81	81

Finally imagine that the government increases both its purchases per head and the tax per head from 20 to 21, respectively. That means, the budget is always balanced. At the beginning, let the economy be in the long-run equilibrium. In the short run, the government action enhances output per head from 100 to 101. In the medium run, public debt does not come into existence. And output per head is still at 101. Put differently, the balanced budget multiplier is unity. Consumption per head is fixed at 72. In the short run, the aggregate of consumption and government purchases per head rises from 92 to 93. In the medium run, it stays at the higher level. Table 3 presents a synopsis.

Table 3
Closed Economy
Increase in Government Purchases and Taxes Per Head

	1	2	3
g	20	21	21
t	20	21	21
y	100	101	101
cc	72	72	72
cc+g	92	93	93

1.3. Endogenous Fiscal Policy

In this section we assume that the government continuously adjusts the budget deficit per head so as to maintain full employment all the time. $\overline{Y}$ denotes full-employment output, hence $\overline{y} = \overline{Y}/N$ is full-employment output per head. The short-run equilibrium can be characterized by a system of three equations:

$$\overline{y} = c(\overline{y} + b - g) + i + g \tag{1}$$

$$\dot{d} = b - nd \tag{2}$$

$$t = g + rd - b \tag{3}$$

Of course this reminds one of exogenous fiscal policy. The only difference is that here output per head becomes exogenous, while the budget deficit per head becomes endogenous. Thus b, $\dot{d}$ and t are endogenous.

What are the principal attributes of the short-run equilibrium? To answer this question, solve equation (1) for the budget deficit per head:

$$b = \frac{(1-c)(\bar{y}-g)-i}{c} \tag{4}$$

First regard a decline in investment per head. To counteract this, the government must increase the budget deficit per head. Much the same applies to a fall in government purchases per head or in the consumption rate. When the government increases the budget deficit per head, then according to the budget identity (3) it reduces the tax per head by the same amount.

The long-run equilibrium is defined by the condition that public debt per head does not change any more $\dot{d} = 0$. That is why the long-run equilibrium can be written in the following way:

$$\bar{y} = c(\bar{y}+b-g)+i+g \tag{5}$$
$$nd = b \tag{6}$$
$$t = g+rd-b \tag{7}$$

Here b, d and t are endogenous.

We come now to the main properties of the long-run equilibrium. Solve (5) for the budget deficit per head:

$$b = \frac{(1-c)(\bar{y}-g)-i}{c} \tag{8}$$

As a finding, the long-run equilibrium is identical to the short-run equilibrium, cf. equation (4). From (6) one can deduce:

$$d = \frac{b}{n} \qquad (9)$$

Let $n > 0$. A reduction in investment per head calls for an increase in the budget deficit per head, so public debt per head accumulates. The same is true of a fall in government purchases per head or in the consumption rate. Further insert (9) into (7) to obtain:

$$t = g + br/n - b \qquad (10)$$

Let $r > n$. Then an increase in the budget deficit per head leads to an increase in the tax per head.

Next we shall probe into stability. Eliminate b in (2) by means of (4) to reach:

$$\dot{d} = \frac{(1-c)(\bar{y}-g)-i}{c} - nd \qquad (11)$$

Then differentiate for d:

$$\frac{\partial \dot{d}}{\partial d} = -n \qquad (12)$$

As an important result, the long-run equilibrium will be stable.

To illuminate this, we shall keep track of the process of adjustment generated by a transitory investment shock. Originally the economy is in the long-run equilibrium. The labour market clears. Let the budget be balanced, so there is no public debt. The tax per head and output per head are invariant. Under these circumstances, investment per head drops. Instantaneously, to prevent unemployment from coming into existence, the government increases the budget deficit per head. That means, it lowers the tax per head, thereby stimulating consumption per head. The net effect is that output per head remains unchanged, hence each worker has still got a job. And what is more, owing to the increase in the budget deficit per head, public debt per head piles up. In order to finance the rise in public interest per head, the government must lift the tax per head.

After a certain span of time, let investment per head return to its original level. Immediately, as a response, the government reduces the budget deficit per head. That is to say, it raises the tax per head, thus restraining consumption per head. On account of the reduction in the budget deficit per head, the trend in public debt per head is reversed. Public debt per head declines, and so do public interest per head as well as the tax per head. As time passes away, the economy tends to a new long-run equilibrium. The labour market still clears. The budget is again balanced, and public debt per head has disappeared from the scene. The tax per head and output per head are uniform.

To conclude, all variables return to their initial levels. Public debt per head eliminates itself, even though the government does not switch to a budget surplus. The reason is that population growth (and technical progress) reduce public debt per head. For the pertinent time paths the reader may wish to refer to figures 1 until 4. Figure 1 contains the autonomous path of investment per head as well as the induced path of the budget deficit per head. Figure 2 exhibits the constant path of output per head. Figure 3 graphs the time structure of public debt per head, and figure 4 that of the tax per head.

Last but not least we assume that the government adjusts both its purchases per head and its deficit per head. Again it does so as to defend full employment all the time. Define $w = g - b$ and let $w = $ const. Then the short-run equilibrium can be described by a system of three equations:

$$\bar{y} = c(\bar{y} - w) + i + g \tag{13}$$

$$\dot{d} = g - w - nd \tag{14}$$

$$t = w + rd \tag{15}$$

In this case $\dot{d}$, g and t are endogenous. The present model is isomorphic to the one we have just studied before, cf. equations (1) until (3).

In summary, the long-run equilibrium will be stable. In this sense, endogenous fiscal policy can be sustained. Essentially this confirms the results obtained for exogenous fiscal policy.

36

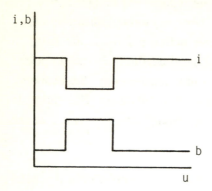

Figure 1
Investment and
Budget Deficit Per Head

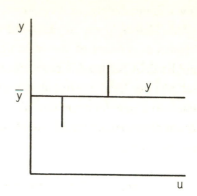

Figure 2
Output Per Head

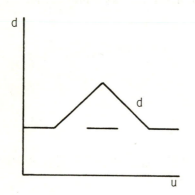

Figure 3
Public Debt Per Head

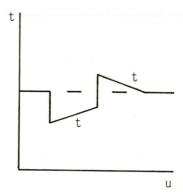

Figure 4
Tax Per Head

1.4. Investment and Capital

The analysis will be conducted within the following framework. Households fix autonomous consumption per head $\bar{c}$ = const as well as the marginal consumption rate c = const. Therefore the consumption function takes the shape $C = \bar{c}N + cY$. Investment I serves to close the gap between the desired stock of capital K* and the actual stock of capital K step by step. Beyond that, investment serves to keep up capital per head. Accordingly the investment function is $I = nK + \lambda(K* - K)$, where $\lambda > 0$ symbolizes the speed of adjustment. The desired capital-output ratio is v = const, so desired capital amounts to $K* = vY$. Putting all pieces together, this yields $I = nK + \lambda(vY - K)$. Investment in turn adds to the stock of capital $\dot{K} = I$. Output equals aggregate demand $Y = C + I$. And labour grows at a uniform rate $\dot{N} = nN$. The momentary equilibrium can be captured by a system of four equations:

$$Y = \bar{c}N + cY + I \tag{1}$$

$$I = nK + \lambda(vY - K) \tag{2}$$

$$\dot{K} = I \tag{3}$$

$$\dot{N} = nN \tag{4}$$

Endogenous are I, $\dot{K}$, $\dot{N}$ and Y.

It proves useful to do the analysis in per capita terms. Equation (1) can be restated as $y = \bar{c} + cy + i$. Capital per head is defined as k = K/N. By virtue of this, equation (2) can be written as $i = nk + \lambda(vy - k)$. Now take the time derivative of capital per head $\dot{k} = \dot{K}/N - K\dot{N}/N^2$ and substitute $\dot{K} = I$ as well as $\dot{N} = nN$ to ascertain $\dot{k} = i - nk$. The momentary equilibrium in per capita terms can be caught by a system of three equations:

$$y = \bar{c} + cy + i \tag{5}$$

$$i = nk + \lambda(vy - k) \tag{6}$$

$$\dot{k} = i - nk \tag{7}$$

Here i, k̇ and y adjust themselves. The momentary equilibrium in per capita terms can be further compressed to a system of two equations:

$$y = \bar{c} + cy + nk + \lambda(vy - k) \tag{8}$$

$$\dot{k} = \lambda(vy - k) \tag{9}$$

In this version k̇ and y are endogenous.

Next the momentary equilibrium will be discussed in greater detail. Solve (8) for output per head:

$$y = \frac{\bar{c} + nk - \lambda k}{1 - c - \lambda v} \tag{10}$$

We postulate $\bar{c} + nk - \lambda k > 0$ and $c + \lambda v < 1$. On this premise, output per head will be positive. Here $c + \lambda v$ denotes the marginal propensity to spend out of income. Judging by (10), an increase in autonomous consumption per head gives rise to an increase in output per head. Besides, let $\lambda > n$. Then an increase in capital per head gives rise to a decline in output per head. The reason is that investment per head comes down as capital per head goes up. An increase in the capital-output ratio gives rise to an increase in output per head. This can be explained as follows. An increase in the capital-output ratio enhances desired capital per head and thus investment per head. Similarly an increase in the growth rate gives rise to an increase in output per head. This can be ascribed to the fact that investment per head moves up as the growth rate moves up.

In the steady state, the motion of capital per head comes to a halt $\dot{k} = 0$. Combine this with equation (9) to get:

$$k = vy \tag{11}$$

Then insert (11) into (8) and solve for output per head:

$$y = \frac{\bar{c}}{1 - c - nv} \tag{12}$$

Provided that $c + nv < 1$, output per head will be positive. An increase in autonomous consumption per head causes an increase in output per head and thus in capital per head, as can be learnt from (11) and (12). Much the same applies to an increase in the capital-output ratio (or in the growth rate, for that matter). Once more imagine an increase in autonomous consumption per head. Will the short-run multiplier be bigger than the long-run multiplier? The comparative evaluation of (10) and (12) yields that, due to $\lambda > n$, the answer is in the affirmative.

What about stability? Eliminate y in (9) with the help of (10) and differentiate for k:

$$\frac{\partial \dot{k}}{\partial k} = \frac{(n - \lambda)\lambda v}{1 - c - \lambda v} - \lambda \tag{13}$$

Owing to $c + nv < 1$, we arrive at $\partial \dot{k} / \partial k < 0$. Put another way, the steady state will be stable.

Next catch a glimpse of the process of adjustment set in motion by an increase in autonomous consumption per head. At the beginning, the economy is in the long-run equilibrium. Investment per head, capital per head and output per head do not change. In this situation, autonomous consumption per head springs up. In the short run, the shock elevates output per head. This in turn pushes up the desired stock of capital per head, investment per head, and output per head. In the medium run, the increase in investment per head contributes to the accumulation of capital per head. But as capital per head grows, investment per head declines. That is why output per head also falls back. Eventually the economy approaches a new long-run equilibrium. Investment per head, capital per head and output per head cease to change.

During transition, a shortage of capital may occur $k < vy$. Firms can manage this by working overtime or running extrashifts. Figure 1 shows the time path of investment per head. At the start, investment per head jumps up. Later on it settles down at an intermediate level. Figure 2 visualizes the accompanying time pattern of capital per head. And the overshooting of investment per head is clearly reflected in the overshooting of output per head, see figure 3.

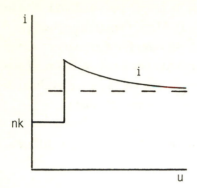

Figure 1
Investment Per Head

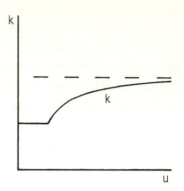

Figure 2
Capital Per Head

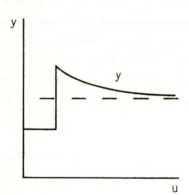

Figure 3
Output Per Head

To elucidate this, take a numerical example with c = 0.6, v = 3, n = 0.02, λ = 0.06 and $\bar{c}$ = 34. Initially the economy is in the steady state. Then autonomous consumption per head rises from 34 to 35. In the short run, as a reaction, investment per head goes up from 6 to 6.8. On those grounds, output per head climbs from 100 to 105. In the medium run, capital per head grows from 300 to 309. Yet investment per head declines from 6.8 to 6.2. And output per head drops from 105 to 103. Table 4 presents an overview.

In summary, there exists a stability condition. Regard for instance an increase in autonomous consumption per head. In the short run, this raises investment per head and output per head. In the medium run, capital per head starts piling up. This in turn lowers investment per head and output per head. It is worth noting that output per head does not fall below its initial level.

Table 4
Investment and Capital Per Head
Increase in Autonomous Consumption Per Head

	1	2	3
$\bar{c}$	34	35	35
y	100	104.6	102.9
i	6	6.8	6.2
k	300	300	308.7

1.5. Capital and Fiscal Policy

The plan of this section is as follows. To begin with, we shall briefly touch upon exogenous fiscal policy. Then we shall throw some more light on endogenous fiscal policy. There government purchases and the budget deficit, in per capita terms respectively, become endogenous.

1) Exogenous fiscal policy. The short-run equilibrium can be encapsulated in a system of four equations:

$$y = c(y + b - g) + nk + \lambda(vy - k) + g \tag{1}$$

$$\dot{k} = \lambda(vy - k) \tag{2}$$

$$\dot{d} = b - nd \tag{3}$$

$$t = g + rd - b \tag{4}$$

Endogenous are $\dot{d}$, $\dot{k}$, t and y. The long-run equilibrium proves to be stable. Consider for example an increase in government purchases and the budget deficit per head. This policy measure enhances output per head. The stock of capital per head accumulates, in spite of the growth in public debt per head.

2) Endogenous fiscal policy. The government continuously adjusts its purchases and its deficit per head so as to safeguard full employment all the time. Define w = g − b and let be w = const. The short-run equilibrium can be characterized by a system of four equations:

$$\bar{y} = c(\bar{y} - w) + nk + \lambda(v\bar{y} - k) + g \tag{5}$$

$$\dot{k} = \lambda(v\bar{y} - k) \tag{6}$$

$$\dot{d} = g - w - nd \tag{7}$$

$$t = w + rd \tag{8}$$

Here g, $\dot{d}$, $\dot{k}$ and t are endogenous. Solve equation (5) for the required level of government purchases per head:

$$g = \bar{y} - c(\bar{y} - w) - nk - \lambda(v\bar{y} - k) \tag{9}$$

In the long-run equilibrium, both public debt per head and capital per head stop moving $\dot{d} = \dot{k} = 0$. This together with (6) delivers:

$$k = v\bar{y} \tag{10}$$

Get rid of k in (5) and regroup:

$$g = (1 - c - nv)\bar{y} + cw \tag{11}$$

Likewise put $\dot{d} = 0$ into (7) and reshuffle terms:

$$d = \frac{g - w}{n} \tag{12}$$

Next we shall inquire into stability, making use of phase diagrams. The short-run equilibrium can be condensed to a system of two differential equations:

$$\dot{d} = \varepsilon(d, k) \tag{13}$$

$$\dot{k} = \eta(d, k) \tag{14}$$

In the present case, equation (14) assumes the shape $\dot{k} = \lambda(v\bar{y} - k)$. Differentiate this for k to check:

$$\frac{\partial \dot{k}}{\partial k} = -\lambda \tag{15}$$

Now set $\dot{k} = \lambda(v\bar{y} - k)$ equal to zero:

$$k = v\bar{y} \tag{16}$$

Correspondingly figure 1 displays the horizontal $\dot{k} = 0$ demarcation line.

Similarly differentiate (7) for d to verify $\partial \dot{d} / \partial d = \partial g / \partial d - n$. Then differentiate (9) for d to get $\partial g / \partial d = 0$. This implies:

$$\frac{\partial \dot{d}}{\partial d} = -n \tag{17}$$

Moreover set $\dot{d} = 0$ in (7) and solve for $d = (g - w)/n$. Further substitute (9) to realize:

$$d = \frac{(1-c)(\bar{y}-w) - nk - \lambda(v\bar{y}-k)}{n} \tag{18}$$

Finally differentiate this for k:

$$\frac{\partial d}{\partial k} = \frac{\lambda - n}{n} > 0 \tag{19}$$

Accordingly figure 1 plots the upward sloping $\dot{d} = 0$ demarcation line. The lesson taught by the phase diagram is that the long-run equilibrium will be stable.

To make this clear, we shall study the process of adjustment kicked off by a transitory investment shock. The exposition will be stylized to a certain extent. Originally the economy is in the steady state. Let the budget be balanced, so there is no public debt. Government purchases per head and the tax per head are invariant. The same holds for output per head. Then, suddenly, investment per head comes down.

Instantaneously, to counteract this, the government increases its purchases and the budget deficit per head, by the same amount respectively. That is why output per head does not respond, so full employment still prevails. The fall in investment per head contributes to the decumulation of capital per head. And the rise in the budget deficit per head contributes to the accumulation of public debt per head. Owing to the swell in public interest per head, the government must lift the tax per head.

After a certain span of time, let investment per head return to its initial level. At once the government reduces its purchases per head and the budget deficit per head. The rise in investment per head contributes to the growth of capital per head. And the fall in the budget deficit per head contributes to the decline in

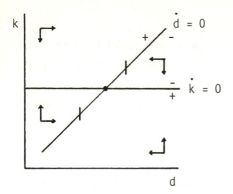

Figure 1
Phase Diagram

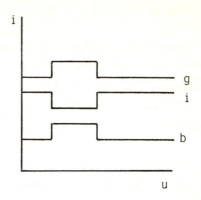

Figure 2
Investment, Government Purchases
and Budget Deficit (Per Head)

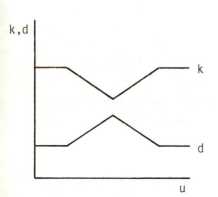

Figure 3
Private Capital and
Public Debt (Per Head)

public debt per head. As public interest per head drops, the government is able to cut the tax per head.

Asymptotically the economy tends to a new steady state, which by the way is identical to the old one. The labour market does always clear. The budget is again balanced, thus public debt has disappeared from the scene. Government purchases and the tax per head are once more constant. And the same is true of output per head.

Figure 2 plots the autonomous path of investment per head as well as the induced paths of government purchases per head and the budget deficit per head. Of course the time patterns of g and b are the mirror images of that of i. Then figure 3 graphs how capital per head and public debt per head move through time.

1.6. Wealth in Consumption Function

Does wealth affect consumption? Is public debt perceived as private wealth? In the current section we shall postulate that the answers to both questions are yes. Let the consumption function be of the type $cc = c(y + rd - t) + \alpha d$, where α d stands for the wealth effect. Then take account of the budget identity $t = g + rd - b$ to get $cc = c(y + b - g) + \alpha d$. That is to say, a unit increase in public debt per head gives rise to an increase in consumption per head of α.

The short-run equilibrium can be represented by a system of two equations:

$$y = c(y + b - g) + \alpha d + i + g \tag{1}$$

$$\dot{d} = b - nd \tag{2}$$

The endogenous variables are $\dot{d}$ and y. Now solve equation (1) for output per head:

$$y = \frac{i+g+c(b-g)+\alpha d}{1-c} \tag{3}$$

Accordingly an increase in public debt per head leads to an increase in output per head. This clearly differs from the conclusions drawn in the standard model, cf. section 1.1.

In the long-run equilibrium, the motion of public debt per head comes to a standstill $\dot{d} = 0$. From this one can derive:

$$d = \frac{b}{n} \tag{4}$$

Further substitute (4) into (3) to accomplish:

$$y = \frac{i+g+c(b-g)+\alpha b/n}{1-c} \tag{5}$$

Consider an increase in government purchases and the budget deficit, in per capita terms respectively. In the short run, this brings up output per head. Then, in the medium run, public debt per head begins to accumulate. Owing to that, consumption per head goes up, so output per head continues to rise. Figure 1 visualizes the part played by the wealth effect.

Finally regard a numerical example with $c = 0.9$, $n = 0.02$ and $\alpha = 0.01$. Here a unit increase in public debt per head causes an increase in consumption per head of 0.01. In this case, the long-run multiplier will be $\partial y/\partial g = 15$. Compare this to the economy without wealth effect $\alpha = 0$, where the long-run multiplier was $\partial y/\partial g = 10$.

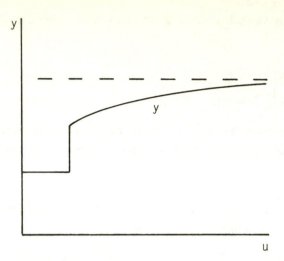

Figure 1
Output Per Head

1.7. Per-Head Approach

In this section, a few comments will be made concerning methodology. In a stationary economy, agents form stationary expectations. For this reason, the trend of output will be constant. In a growing economy, on the other hand, agents form growth expectations. On these grounds, the trend of output will be growing.

First catch a glimpse of a stationary economy. Take an extremely simple model:

$$Y = cY + I \tag{1}$$

Let investment be autonomous I = const, and let consumption vary in proportion to income c = const. Of course the solution to this model is:

$$Y = \frac{I}{1-c} \tag{2}$$

As a result, output is constant, too.

We proceed now to a growing economy. Looking backward, labour supply (in efficiency units) has grown at a rate of say 2% year after year. As a trend, output per head of labour supply has been constant. Therefore firms expect that this trend will continue. That is why they fix their investment in per capita terms. As a consequence, output per head will in fact be constant. To a certain extent, this seems to be a case of self-fulfilling expectations. Quite naturally, business cycles are superimposed on this trend. During boom, investment per head goes up, so output per head goes up. During slump, conversely, investment per head comes down, so output per head comes down.

Consider a very simple model:

$$Y = cY + iN \tag{3}$$

$$\dot{N} = nN \tag{4}$$

i = const denotes autonomous investment per head of labour supply, N is labour supply, and n = const is the growth rate of labour supply. Here $\dot{N}$ and Y are endogenous. It proves useful to restate the model in per capita terms:

$$y = cy + i \qquad (5)$$

In this version y is endogenous. Solve equation (5) for output per head:

$$y = \frac{i}{1-c} \qquad (6)$$

As a finding, output per head is constant, too.

To better understand the working of the model, take a numerical example with c = 0.9 and n = 0.1. Table 5 shows the time paths in absolute terms. Column I gives the exogenous path of investment, Y is the endogenous path of output, N is the exogenous path of labour supply, and L is the endogenous path of labour demand (which is based on a production function with fixed coefficients L/Y = const). In period 4 the economy is hit by a shock, to the effect that investment stagnates. Due to that, output and labour demand stagnate as well. Labour supply, however, does not stagnate.

Table 6 presents the corresponding time paths in per capita terms (i.e. per head of labour supply, not labour demand). Column i gives the exogenous path of investment per head, y is the endogenous path of output per head, and 1 − L/N is the rate of unemployment. In period 4, investment per head declines. This in turn lowers output per head, thereby raising the rate of unemployment.

Similarly table 7 displays the time paths in terms of growth rates, where the hat symbolizes the growth rate $\hat{I} = \dot{I}/I$. Column $\hat{I}$ gives the exogenous growth rate of investment, $\hat{Y}$ is the endogenous growth rate of output, $\hat{N}$ is the exogenous growth rate of labour supply, and $\hat{L}$ is the endogenous growth rate of labour demand. In period 4, the growth rate of investment is zero. Owing to that, the growth rates of output and labour demand are also zero. But the growth rate of labour supply stays at 0.1.

Table 5
Time Paths in Absolute Terms

u	I	Y	N	L
1	10	100	1	1
2	11	110	1.1	1.1
3	12.1	121	1.21	1.21
4	12.1	121	1.33	1.21
5	13.3	133	1.46	1.33
6	14.6	146	1.61	1.46

Table 6
Time Paths in Per Capita Terms

u	i	y	1-L/N
1	10	100	0
2	10	100	0
3	10	100	0
4	9.1	91	0.09
5	9.1	91	0.09
6	9.1	91	0.09

Table 7

Time Paths in Growth Rates

u	$\hat{I}$	$\hat{Y}$	$\hat{N}$	$\hat{L}$
1	0.1	0.1	0.1	0.1
2	0.1	0.1	0.1	0.1
3	0.1	0.1	0.1	0.1
4	0	0	0.1	0
5	0.1	0.1	0.1	0.1
6	0.1	0.1	0.1	0.1

Figures 1 until 3 reveal the time paths occasioned by an investment shock. The underlying economy can be either stationary or growing. Let us begin with a stationary economy. Figure 1 exhibits the autonomous path of investment and the induced path of output. We come now to a growing economy. Figure 2 plots the autonomous path of investment and the induced path of output, on a semilogarithmic scale, respectively. Correspondingly, figure 3 graphs the autonomous path of investment per head and the induced path of output per head. The figures mark the difference between an investment shock in a stationary economy and in a growing economy.

To summarize, in a stationary economy, the trend of output is constant. During boom output rises, and during slump it falls. In a growing economy, on the other hand, the trend of output per head is constant. During boom output per head rises, and during slump it falls.

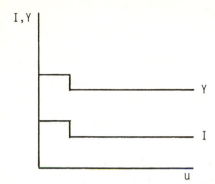

Figure 1
Investment and Output
(Stationary Economy)

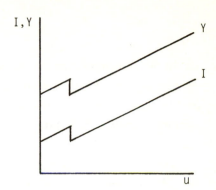

Figure 2
Investment and Output
(Growing Economy)

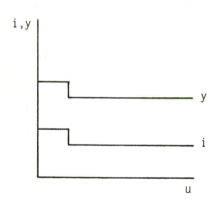

Figure 3
Investment and Output Per Head
(Growing Economy)

1.8. Monetary Policy

In the preceding sections, the interest rate was supposed to be exogenous. In the current section, the interest rate becomes endogenous. In doing this, we shall proceed in two steps. At first we address an economy without public sector, and then we introduce the public sector, laying special emphasis on public debt.

1) Economy without public sector. We start right out with the goods market. Households consume a certain fraction of their income $C = cY$ with $c = $ const. Investment per head is a decreasing function of the interest rate $ii = i - \gamma r$, where i denotes autonomous investment per head and $\gamma = $ const is the interest rate sensitivity. Multiplying investment per head by labour supply gives the total of investment $I = iN - \gamma rN$. Output is determined by aggregate demand $Y = C + I$.

We turn now to the money market. Money demand per head is an increasing function of income per head and a decreasing function of the interest rate $\kappa y - \delta r$. Here $\kappa > 0$ stands for income sensitivity, and $\delta > 0$ for interest sensitivity. Multiplying money demand per head by labour supply gives money demand $L = \kappa Y - \delta rN$. The central bank fixes the money supply in per capita terms $m = $ const. Multiplying money supply per head by labour supply gives money supply $M = mN$. The money market clears $M = L$.

The short-run equilibrium can be written as a system of three equations:

$$Y = cY + iN - \gamma rN \tag{1}$$

$$mN = \kappa Y - \delta rN \tag{2}$$

$$\dot{N} = nN \tag{3}$$

Here r, $\dot{N}$ and Y are endogenous. It is again helpful to implement the analysis in per capita terms. The short-run equilibrium in per capita terms can be described by a system of two equations:

$$y = cy + i - \gamma r \tag{4}$$

$$m = \kappa y - \delta r \tag{5}$$

In this version r and y are endogenous. Equation (4) yields the downward sloping IS curve, see figure 1. In full analogy, equation (5) yields the upward sloping LM curve.

What are the characteristics of the short-run equilibrium? To answer this question, get rid of r in (4) by means of (5) and rearrange:

$$y = \frac{i + \gamma m / \delta}{1 - c + \gamma \kappa / \delta} \tag{6}$$

An increase in autonomous investment per head shifts the IS curve to the right, see figure 1. The shock raises both output per head and the interest rate, as can be learnt from the diagram. Likewise an increase in money supply per head displaces the LM curve to the right. The policy measure brings up output per head by cutting down the interest rate.

2) Economy with public sector (public debt). The short-run equilibrium can be captured by a system of three equations:

$$y = c(y + b - g) + i - \gamma r + g \tag{7}$$

$$m = \kappa y - \delta r \tag{8}$$

$$\dot{d} = b - nd \tag{9}$$

In this case $\dot{d}$, r and y are endogenous. What about the attributes of the short-run equilibrium? Eliminate r in (7) by making use of (8) to establish output per head:

$$y = \frac{i + g + c(b - g) + \gamma m / \delta}{1 - c + \gamma \kappa / \delta} \tag{10}$$

In the long-run equilibrium, public debt per head ceases to move $\dot{d} = 0$. This provides:

$$d = \frac{b}{n} \tag{11}$$

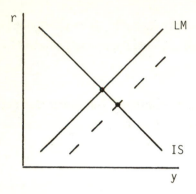

Figure 1
Monetary Policy

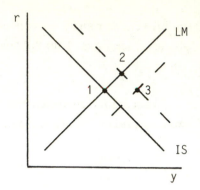

Figure 2
Fiscal Policy

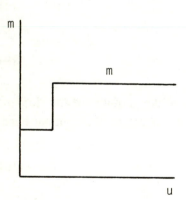

Figure 3
Endogenous Money Supply Per Head

In addition, the long-run equilibrium of output per head coincides with the short-run equilibrium, cf. equation (10).

To illustrate this, we keep track of the process of adjustment kicked off by a fiscal expansion. Initially the economy rests in the steady state. Public debt per head is invariant. In figure 2, the steady state lies in point 1. In this situation, the government increases its purchases per head and the budget deficit per head. In the diagram, the IS curve travels to the right. In the short run, the policy measure enhances output per head and the interest rate. In the diagram, the momentary equilibrium is marked as 2.

In the medium run, the increase in the budget deficit per head contributes to the accumulation of public debt per head. Output per head and the interest rate, however, do not respond. In the diagram nothing happens. In due course, the economy approximates a new steady state. Public debt per head stops piling up. In the diagram, the new steady state lies in point 2. To conclude, there is a one-time jump in output per head and the interest rate. The bidding up of the interest rate, on its part, depresses investment per head. But the accelerator, which has not been built into the model, would have it that the lift in output per head elevated investment per head.

Over and above that, monetary policy can keep the interest rate constant, if it wishes to do so. This assumption has been made throughout the current chapter. To exemplify this, have once more a look at a fiscal expansion. At the beginning, the economy rests in the long-term equilibrium. Public debt per head is uniform. In figure 2, the long-term equilibrium lies in point 1. Under these circumstances, the government increases its purchases per head and the budget deficit per head. In the diagram, the IS curve shifts to the right. To prevent the interest rate from going up, the central bank augments the money supply per head. In the diagram, the LM curve shifts to the right as well. In the short term, this policy mix brings up output per head. In the diagram, the short-term equilibrium is marked as 3.

In the intermediate term, on account of the increase in the budget deficit per head, public debt per head starts to grow. Yet this does not affect output per head and the interest rate, so there is no need for the central bank to intervene. In the diagram nothing occurs. With the lapse of time, the economy converges to a new long-term equilibrium. Public debt per head ceases to move. In the diagram, the long-term equilibrium lies still in point 3. Figure 3 visualizes the time path of monetary policy that is required to do the job.

1.9. Money Finance of Budget Deficit

So far, we posited debt finance of the budget deficit. Now, instead, we posit money finance of the budget deficit. The short-run equilibrium can be represented by a system of five equations:

$$Y = c(Y - tN) + iN - \gamma rN + gN \tag{1}$$

$$M = \kappa Y - \delta rN \tag{2}$$

$$\dot{M} = bN \tag{3}$$

$$tN = gN - bN \tag{4}$$

$$\dot{N} = nN \tag{5}$$

Equation (1) is the goods market equation, and equation (2) is the money market equation. Equation (3) has it that the budget deficit adds to the quantity of money. Equation (4) is the budget identity, and equation (5) refers to labour growth. The endogenous variables are r, t, $\dot{M}$, $\dot{N}$ and Y.

It proves useful to conduct the analysis in per capita terms. m = M/N symbolizes money supply per head. Now take the time derivative of money supply per head $\dot{m} = \dot{M}/N - M\dot{N}/N^2$. Then pay attention to equations (3) and (5), which gives $\dot{m} = b - nm$. Thus the short-run equilibrium in per capita terms can be characterized by a system of four equations:

$$y = c(y - t) + i - \gamma r + g \tag{6}$$

$$m = \kappa y - \delta r \tag{7}$$

$$\dot{m} = b - nm \tag{8}$$

$$t = g - b \tag{9}$$

In this version, $\dot{m}$, r, t and y are endogenous.

Combine equations (6), (7) and (9) to reach output per head:

$$y = \frac{i + g + c(b - g) + \gamma m / \delta}{1 - c + \gamma \kappa / \delta} \tag{10}$$

This is identical to the results obtained under debt finance. In the long-run equilibrium, money supply per head does not change any more $\dot{m} = 0$. From this one can deduce:

$$m = \frac{b}{n} \tag{11}$$

Evidently an increase in the budget deficit per head raises money supply per head. And what about stability? Differentiate (8) for m to get:

$$\frac{\partial \dot{m}}{\partial m} = -n \tag{12}$$

Let be $n > 0$. As an outcome, the long-run equilibrium will be stable.

At last we trace out the process of adjustment set in motion by a fiscal expansion. Originally the economy is in the steady state. Particularly, money supply per head is constant. In figure 1, the steady state is situated in point 1. Against this background, the government increases its purchases per head and the budget deficit per head. In the diagram, the IS curve goes to the right. In the short run, the policy measure enhances both output per head and the interest rate, while the tax per head stays fixed. In the diagram, the momentary equilibrium is marked as 2.

In the medium run, the increase in the budget deficit per head contributes to the accumulation of money supply per head. In the diagram, the LM curve goes to the right step by step. The interest rate drops, which advances output per head.

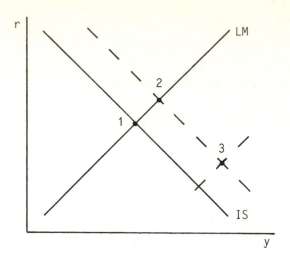

Figure 1
Money Finance of Budget Deficit

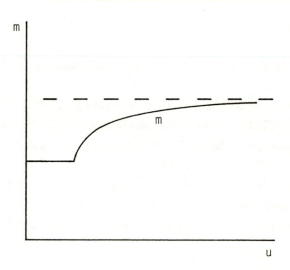

Figure 2
Endogenous Money Supply Per Head

This leaves no impact on the tax per head. As time passes away, the economy approaches a new steady state. Money supply per head comes to a halt. In the diagram, the steady state is situated in point 3. Beyond that, figure 2 depicts the trajectory of money supply per head that is induced by the fiscal expansion.

In summary, the long-run equilibrium will be stable. Imagine the government raises its purchases per head and the budget deficit per head. In the short run, this lifts output per head. Then, in the medium run, money supply per head begins to grow, thereby lifting output per head a second time. In this sense, money finance of the budget deficit can be sustained.

1.10. Crowding Out

1) Fiscal expansion at full employment. Let $\bar{y}$ denote full-employment output per head. The short-run equilibrium can be written as a system of two equations:

$$\bar{y} = c(\bar{y} + b - g) + i + g \tag{1}$$
$$\dot{k} = i - nk \tag{2}$$

Here i and $\dot{k}$ are endogenous. Regard for instance an increase in government purchases per head and the budget deficit per head $\Delta b = \Delta g$. At full employment, this policy measure crowds out investment per head one to one $\Delta i = -\Delta g$. This in turn contributes to the decumulation of capital per head round by round.

2) Fiscal expansion at capacity constraint. Let π symbolize capital productivity, so πk is capacity output per head. The short-run equilibrium can again be described by a system of two equations:

$$\pi k = c(\pi k + b - g) + i + g \tag{3}$$

$$\dot{k} = i - nk \tag{4}$$

In this version, too, i and $\dot{k}$ are endogenous. Now suppose that the government raises its purchases and its deficit, in per capita terms respectively $\Delta b = \Delta g$. At capacity constraint, this government action displaces investment per head one to one $\Delta i = -\Delta g$. On its part, this reduces capital per head and thus capacity output per head. That is why investment per head continues to fall, thereby accelerating the decline in both capital per head and capacity output per head. This process repeats itself period by period.

What about stability? Solve equation (3) for investment per head $i = \pi k - c(\pi k + b - g) - g$ and put this into equation (4):

$$\dot{k} = \pi k - c(\pi k + b - g) - g - nk \tag{5}$$

Then differentiate (5) for k:

$$\frac{\partial \dot{k}}{\partial k} = (1-c)\pi - n \tag{6}$$

Take a numerical example with $c = 0.9$, $n = 0.02$ and $\pi = 0.33$, which yields $\partial \dot{k} / \partial k = 0.013$. In this case, the long-run equilibrium will be unstable. As a consequence, the fiscal expansion squeezes capital per head down to zero. Ultimately, the economy must break down. For a deeper analysis see Carlberg (1992, 1995).

1.11. Fixed Deficit Rate

In the preceding sections, we assumed a fixed deficit per head. In the current section, instead, we shall assume a fixed deficit rate. Apart from this we shall take the same avenue as before. Let us begin with the public sector. The government spends a certain fraction of national income on goods and services $G = gY$ with purchase rate $g = $ const. Moreover the government borrows a specified proportion of national income $B = bY$ with deficit rate $b = $ const. The budget deficit in turn adds to public debt $\dot{D} = B$. The government pays the interest rate $r = $ const on public debt D, so public interest amounts to rD. In addition, the government imposes a tax at the flat rate $t = $ const on both national income and public interest $T = t(Y + rD)$. The government budget identity gives the required level of taxation $T = G + rD - B$. Assembling all component parts, we reach $t(Y + rD) = gY + rD - bY$. Here b and g are exogenous, while t is endogenous.

We come now to the goods market. Disposable income can be defined as national income and public interest, net after tax respectively $Y_d = Y + rD - T$. Insert $T = G + rD - B$ to get $Y_d = Y + B - G$. Further note $B = bY$ and $G = gY$ to find $Y_d = (1 + b - g)Y$. Households consume a fixed share of disposable income $C = cY_d$ or $C = c(1 + b - g)Y$ with $c = $ const. Firms fix investment on a per capita basis $I = iN$ with $i = $ const. Output coincides with aggregate demand $Y = C + I + G$. From this one can conclude $Y = c(1 + b - g)Y + iN + gY$.

In full analogy, the short-run equilibrium can be represented by a system of four equations:

$$Y = c(1 + b - g)Y + iN + gY \tag{1}$$

$$\dot{D} = bY \tag{2}$$

$$t(Y + rD) = gY + rD - bY \tag{3}$$

$$\dot{N} = nN \tag{4}$$

Here t, $\dot{D}$, $\dot{N}$ and Y are endogenous. It is helpful to do the analysis in per capita terms. Accordingly the short-run equilibrium (1) until (4) can be compressed to a system of three equations:

$$y = c(1+b-g)y + i + gy \tag{5}$$

$$\dot{d} = by - nd \tag{6}$$

$$t(y+rd) = gy + rd - by \tag{7}$$

In this version $\dot{d}$, t and y are endogenous.

Solve equation (5) for output per head:

$$y = \frac{i}{1 - c(1+b-g) - g} \tag{8}$$

Judging by equation (8), an increase in investment per head leads to an increase in output per head. What is more, the same holds for a simultaneous increase in the purchase rate and the deficit rate $\Delta b = \Delta g$. We proceed next to stability. Differentiate (6) for d, paying attention to $\partial y / \partial d = 0$:

$$\frac{\partial \dot{d}}{\partial d} = -n \tag{9}$$

As a corollary, the long-run equilibrium will be stable.

Imagine that the government raises both its purchase rate and its deficit rate. In the short run, this enhances output per head. Then, in the medium run, public debt per head starts to build up. This, however, has no influence on output per head. Put another way, there is a one-time jump in output per head. Essentially this confirms the results obtained in the standard model, cf. section 1.1.

2. Fixed Tax Per Head

2.1. Exogenous Fiscal Policy

When the government fixes the tax per head then, according to the budget identity, it must adjust the deficit per head. First have a closer look at the public sector. The government fixes its purchases of goods and services on a per capita basis $g = \text{const}$. Multiplying government purchases per head by labour supply gives government purchases $G = gN$. Likewise the government fixes taxation on a per capita basis $t = \text{const}$. Multiplying the tax per head by labour supply gives tax revenue $T = tN$. The government pays the interest rate $r = \text{const}$ on public debt D, so public interest totals rD. The budget deficit can be defined as the excess of government purchases and public interest over tax revenue $B = G + rD - T$. The budget deficit in turn adds to public debt $\dot{D} = B$. Putting all pieces together, we arrive at $\dot{D} = gN + rD - tN$.

The next point refers to the goods market. Disposable income is factor income augmented by public interest and diminished by taxation $Y_d = Y + rD - T$. Households consume a certain fraction of disposable income $C = cY_d$ with $c = \text{const}$. And firms fix investment on a per capita basis $I = iN$ with $i = \text{const}$. Output is controlled by aggregate demand $Y = C + I + G$. This implies $Y = c(Y + rD - tN) + iN + gN$.

Resting on this groundwork, the short-run equilibrium can be characterized by a system of three equations:

$$Y = c(Y + rD - tN) + iN + gN \tag{1}$$

$$\dot{D} = gN + rD - tN \tag{2}$$

$$\dot{N} = nN \tag{3}$$

Here $\dot{D}$, $\dot{N}$ and Y are endogenous. It proves useful to carry out the investigation in per capita terms. In this way, the short-run equilibrium simplifies to a system of two equations:

$$y = c(y + rd - t) + i + g \qquad (4)$$

$$\dot{d} = g + rd - t - nd \qquad (5)$$

In this version $\dot{d}$ and y are endogenous.

What are the chief properties of the short-run equilibrium? Solve equation (4) for output per head:

$$y = \frac{i + g + c(rd - t)}{1 - c} \qquad (6)$$

Obviously an increase in government purchases per head brings up output per head. Much the same applies to an increase in public debt per head.

Now we shall probe into stability. Differentiate the equation of motion (5) for d to verify:

$$\frac{\partial \dot{d}}{\partial d} = r - n \qquad (7)$$

Here two cases can occur. If the interest rate falls short of the growth rate, the long-run equilibrium will be stable. On the other hand, it the interest rate exceeds the growth rate, the long-run equilibrium will be unstable. Empirically speaking the interest rate surpasses the growth rate, so the long-run equilibrium will in fact be unstable.

Finally we shall keep track of the process of adjustment induced by an increase in government purchases per head. At the beginning let the economy be in a long-run equilibrium without public debt. The budget is balanced, and output per head does not move. Under these circumstances, the government increases its purchases per head, holding the tax per head constant. In the short run, this action lifts output (and employment) per head. The budget gets into deficit.

In the medium run, owing to the budget deficit per head, public debt per head comes into existence, accumulating period by period. The government has to make more and more interest payments per head. This enlarges disposable income per head, thereby stimulating consumption per head and output per head. In

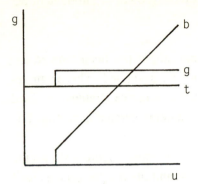

Figure 1
Increase in Government
Purchases Per Head

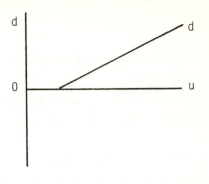

Figure 2
Public Debt Per Head

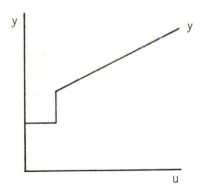

Figure 3
Output Per Head

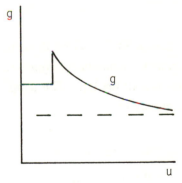

Figure 4
Endogenous Fiscal Policy

order to finance the growth of public interest per head, the government must raise the budget deficit per head, which in turn speeds up the growth of public debt per head.

In the long run, both public debt per head and output per head tend to explode. In this sense, a fixed tax per head cannot be sustained. This is in remarkable contrast to the conclusions drawn for the alternative strategy. A fixed deficit per head can always be sustained, as has been demonstrated in section 1.1.

Figures 1 until 3 illuminate the accompanying time paths. Figure 1 shows the autonomous paths of government purchases per head and the tax per head as well as the induced path of the budget deficit per head. The budget deficit per head grows without limits. This is clearly reflected in the time structure of public debt per head, see figure 2. Figure 3 depicts the endogenous path of output per head. In the short run, output per head springs up. Then, in the medium run, it continues to rise without bounds.

2.2. Endogenous Fiscal Policy

The analysis will be implemented within the following framework. The government continuously adjusts its purchases per head so as to defend full employment all the time. The temporary equilibrium can be caught by a system of two equations:

$$\overline{y} = c(\overline{y} + rd - t) + i + g \tag{1}$$
$$\dot{d} = g + rd - t - nd \tag{2}$$

Here $\dot{d}$ and g are endogenous. Now solve equation (1) for government purchases per head:

$$g = \overline{y} - c(\overline{y} + rd - t) - i \tag{3}$$

From this it is evident that a decline in investment per head must be offset by an increase in government purchases per head.

Further we shall discuss stability. Substitute (3) into (2) and rearrange:

$$\dot{d} = (1-c)(\bar{y}+rd-t)-i-nd \tag{4}$$

Then differentiate (4) for d to ascertain:

$$\frac{\partial \dot{d}}{\partial d} = (1-c)r-n \tag{5}$$

Hence we reach a different stability condition. If $(1 - c)\, r < n$, the permanent equilibrium will be stable. Conversely, if $(1 - c)\, r > n$, the permanent equilibrium will be unstable. To assess this condition, take a numerical example with $c = 0.9$, $n = 0.02$ and $r = 0.04$. This provides $(1 - c)\, r = 0.004$. From the empirical point of view, the condition seems to be fulfilled. Therefore the permanent equilibrium will be stable. As a result, endogenous fiscal policy can be sustained. This is in clear opposition to exogenous fiscal policy, where the permanent equilibrium turned out to be unstable. That means, endogenous fiscal policy increases (the likelihood of) stability.

In the permanent equilibrium, public debt per head ceases to move $\dot{d} = 0$. Combine this with equation (4) and reshuffle terms:

$$d = \frac{(1-c)(\bar{y}-t)-i}{n-(1-c)r} \tag{6}$$

Let the stability condition $(1 - c)\, r < n$ be fulfilled. Then a drop in investment per head causes a lift in public debt per head, as can be seen from (6). Moreover, equation (3) together with equation (6) yield the permanent equilibrium of government purchases per head. Regard for instance a decline in investment per head. In the short term, leaning against the wind, the government raises its purchases per head. Then, in the intermediate term, public debt per head starts to grow. To compensate for this, the government lowers its purchases per head.

By the way, do government purchases per head fall below their initial level? To solve this problem, differentiate (3) for i to get $\partial g/\partial i = - cr\partial d/\partial i - 1$. Similarly differentiate (6) for i to get $\partial d/\partial i = - 1/[n - (1 - c)r]$. Then dispense with $\partial d/\partial i$ and regroup:

$$\frac{\partial g}{\partial i} = \frac{r - n}{n - (1 - c)r} \tag{7}$$

Let $r > n$. Thus we find $\partial g/\partial i > 0$. In the long term, a cut in investment per head requires a cut in government purchases per head. That is to say, government purchases per head indeed fall below their initial level. Correspondingly figure 4 reveals the endogenous path of government purchases per head.

To shed some more light on this process, consider a numerical example with $c = 0.9$, $t = 0.2$, $n = 0.02$, $r = 0.04$, $i = 8$ and $\bar{y} = 100$. Being in the long-term equilibrium, the economy is hit by a shock. Investment per head comes down from 8 to 7. In the short term, the government must increase its purchases per head from 20 to 21. Then, in the intermediate term, public debt per head comes into existence, rising continuously from 0 to 60. For that reason, the government must reduce its purchases per head from 21 to 19, step by step. In the short term, this leaves no impact on consumption per head $cc = 72$. Then, in the intermediate term, consumption per head improves to 74. Finally take the sum of consumption and government purchases, in per capita terms respectively. In the short term, the sum goes up from 92 to 93. And in the intermediate term, it stays at the higher level. Table 8 offers a synopsis.

Table 8
Fixed Tax Per Head
Endogenous Fiscal Policy

	1	2	3
i	8	7	7
g	20	21	19.3
y	100	100	100
d	0	0	59.5
cc	72	72	73.7
cc+g	92	93	93

3. Fixed Tax Rate

3.1. Exogenous Fiscal Policy

We start right out with the public sector. The government fixes its purchases of goods and services on a per capita basis g = const. Multiplying government purchases per head by labour supply gives government purchases G = gN. In addition the government imposes a tax at the flat rate t = const on both factor income and public interest T = t(Y + rD). Government purchases plus public interest minus tax revenue gives the budget deficit B = G + rD − T. The budget deficit in turn adds to public debt $\dot{D}$ = B. Fitting the puzzle together, we achieve $\dot{D} = gN + rD - t(Y + rD)$.

Next a few words will be said with respect to the goods market. Disposable income can be defined as the sum of factor income and public interest, net after tax respectively $Y_d = Y + rD - T$. Households consume a specified proportion of disposable income $C = cY_d$ with c = const. And firms fix investment on a per capita basis I = iN with i = const. Output agrees with aggregate demand Y = C + I + G. From this one can extract Y = c(1 − t)(Y + rD) + iN + gN.

The short-run equilibrium can be encapsulated in a system of three equations:

$$Y = c(1-t)(Y+rD) + iN + gN \tag{1}$$

$$\dot{D} = gN + rD - t(Y+rD) \tag{2}$$

$$\dot{N} = nN \tag{3}$$

Here $\dot{D}$, $\dot{N}$ and Y are endogenous. In per capita terms, the short-run equilibrium can be compressed to a system of two equations:

$$y = c(1-t)(y+rd) + i + g \tag{4}$$

$$\dot{d} = g + rd - t(y+rd) - nd \tag{5}$$

In this version, $\dot{d}$ and y are endogenous.

What are the salient features of the short-run equilibrium? Solve equation (4) for output per head:

$$y = \frac{i+g+c(1-t)rd}{1-c(1-t)} \tag{6}$$

Accordingly an increase in investment per head gives rise to an increase in output per head. The same applies to an increase in government purchases per head (or, for that matter, in public debt per head).

The short-run equilibrium can be further condensed to a single differential equation $\dot{d} = \varepsilon(d)$. Substitute (6) into (5) and regroup:

$$\dot{d} = \frac{(1-c)(1-t)(g+rd)-ti}{1-c(1-t)} - nd \tag{7}$$

What about stability? Differentiate (7) for d:

$$\frac{\partial \dot{d}}{\partial d} = \frac{(1-c)(1-t)r}{1-c(1-t)} - n \tag{8}$$

From this one can derive the stability condition:

$$(1-c)(1-t)r < \left[1-c(1-t)\right]n \tag{9}$$

Take a numerical example with $c = 0.9$, $t = 0.2$, $n = 0.02$ and $r = 0.04$. In this case, the stability condition will be fulfilled $(1 - c)(1 - t)r = 0.032 < [1 - c(1 - t)]n = 0.0056$. Speaking more generally, there exists a critical level of the consumption rate $c' = 0.75$. If the consumption rate exceeds 0.75, the long-run equilibrium will be stable. The other way round, if the consumption rate falls short of 0.75, the long-run equilibrium will be unstable. Henceforth, let this condition be satisfied.

In the long-run equilibrium, public debt per head comes to a halt $\dot{d} = 0$. Insert this into (7) to accomplish:

$$d = \frac{(1-c)(1-t)g - ti}{[1-c(1-t)]n - (1-c)(1-t)r} \tag{10}$$

An increase in investment per head causes a reduction in public debt per head. And an increase in government purchases per head causes an increase in public debt per head.

First suppose that the government raises its purchases per head. In the short run, this enhances output per head. Then, in the medium run, public debt per head begins to grow, so output per head continues to rise. Second regard an increase in investment per head. In the short run, this elevates output per head. Then, in the medium run, public debt per head begins to decline, thereby depressing output per head.

Now we shall take a closer look at the budget deficit. In the short-run equilibrium it holds $\dot{D} = B$. It is convenient to transform this into per capita terms $\dot{d} = b - nd$, where b denotes the budget deficit per head. Compare this with (7) to realize:

$$b = \frac{(1-c)(1-t)(g + rd) - ti}{1 - c(1-t)} \tag{11}$$

By virtue of (11), figure 1 shows the budget deficit per head as a function of public debt per head. Besides, figure 1 portrays the nd ray. Stability implies $\partial b / \partial d < n$. In the long-run equilibrium we have:

$$b = nd \tag{12}$$

which in the diagram is marked by the point of intersection.

Beyond that imagine an increase in government purchases per head. How does this affect public debt per head? Initially let the economy be in the long-run equilibrium, which in figure 2 is represented by point 1. Then government purchases per head go up. Correspondingly, the b line shifts upwards. The short-run equilibrium lies in point 2. Eventually the economy reaches a new long-run equilibrium, which in the diagram is situated in point 3. More exactly, b symbolizes the actual budget deficit per head, while nd is the budget deficit per head that

76

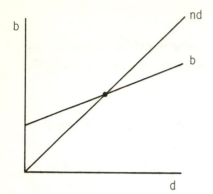

Figure 1
Budget Deficit Per Head

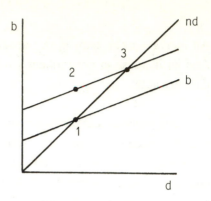

Figure 2
Increase in
Government Purchases Per Head

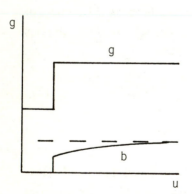

Figure 3
Government Purchases and
Budget Deficit Per Head

is required to keep public debt per head constant. In the short run, the budget deficit per head surpasses the required level, so public debt per head builds up. To conclude, let the government increase its purchases per head. In the short run, this measure drives up the budget deficit per head. Then, in the medium run, public debt per head piles up. On those grounds the budget deficit per head continues to move up.

At this stage, the full dynamics of a fiscal expansion can be studied in a coherent way. At the outset, the economy is in a long-run equilibrium without public debt. The budget is balanced, and output per head does not move. Under these circumstances, the government increases its purchases per head, holding the tax rate constant. In the short run, this action lifts output per head. And the budget registers a deficit.

In the medium run, the budget deficit per head contributes to the accumulation of public debt per head. The swell in public interest per head enlarges disposable income per head, thus stimulating consumption per head and output per head. In order to cover the swell in public interest per head, the government must raise the budget deficit per head. Thanks to the growth in both public interest per head and output per head, the government collects more and more tax revenue per head. Asymptotically the economy converges to a new long-run equilibrium. The budget deficit per head and public debt per head stop adjusting. And output per head does not move any more.

Figures 3, 4 and 5 contain the relevant time paths. Figure 3 visualizes the autonomous path of government purchases per head as well as the induced path of the budget deficit per head. In the short run, the budget deficit per head springs up. Then, in the intermediate run, it keeps on going up. This is clearly reflected in the time path of public debt per head, see figure 4. Figure 5 depicts the trajectory of output per head. In the short run, the fiscal expansion enhances output per head. Then, in the medium run, output per head continues to climb.

In summary, a fixed tax rate can possibly be sustained. This is in contradistinction to a fixed tax per head, which cannot be sustained, cf. section 2.1.

Coming to an end, take a numerical example with $c = 0.9$, $t = 0.2$, $n = 0.02$, $r = 0.04$, $i = 8$ and $g = 20$. First assume that the government increases its purcha-

78

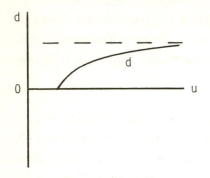

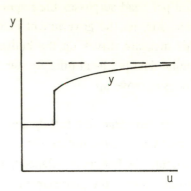

Figure 4
Increase in
Government Purchases Per Head

Figure 5
Increase in
Government Purchases Per Head

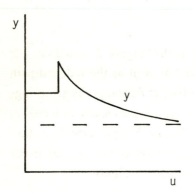

Figure 6
Increase in
Investment Per Head

ses per head from 20 to 21. In the short run, this boosts output per head from 100 to 104. Then, in the medium run, public debt per head comes into existence, growing slowly from 0 to 33. That is why output per head keeps on moving upwards until it reaches 107. In the short run, there is a jump in the budget deficit per head from 0 to 0.3. Then, in the medium run, it continues to rise to 0.7. Table 9 presents an overview.

Table 9
Fixed Tax Rate
Increase in Government Purchases Per Head

	1	2	3
g	20	21	21
y	100	103.6	107
d	0	0	33.3
b	0	0.3	0.7

Here a comment is in place concerning the speed of adjustment. As a finding, the half-life of this process is 81 years. That means, in period 81 public debt per head totals 16.69. So this is a very slow process.

Second consider an increase in investment per head from 8 to 9, letting government purchases per head be back at 20. In the short run, the disturbance brings up output per head from 100 to 104. Then, in the medium run, public debt per head declines from 0 to − 83. Here negative public debt signifies that the government buys private bonds. For that reason, output per head shrinks from 104 to 95. Table 10 offers a synopsis. And figure 6 reveals the associated time path of output per head. In the medium run, the upward trend of output per head is reversed. In the long run, it falls well below its initial level.

Table 10
Fixed Tax Rate
Increase in Investment Per Head

	1	2	3
i	8	9	9
y	100	103.6	95
d	0	0	− 83.3

3.2. Endogenous Fiscal Policy

This section relies on the premise that the government continuously adapts its purchases per head so as to maintain full employment all the time. A similar approach has been pursued by Cohen and de Leeuw (1980). They posit a stationary economy and derive a stability condition.

The short-run equilibrium of a growing economy can be written as a system of two equations:

$$\bar{y} = c(1-t)(\bar{y}+rd)+i+g \tag{1}$$

$$\dot{d} = g+rd - t(\bar{y}+rd) - nd \tag{2}$$

Here $\dot{d}$ and g are endogenous. Solve equation (1) for the required level of government purchases per head:

$$g = \bar{y} - c(1-t)(\bar{y}+rd) - i \tag{3}$$

Apparently a reduction in investment per head calls for an increase in government purchases per head. And an increase in public debt per head calls for a reduction in government purchases per head.

The short-run equilibrium can be further compressed to a single differential equation. Eliminate g in (2) by making use of (3) and reshuffle terms:

$$\dot{d} = (1-c)(1-t)(\bar{y}+rd) - i - nd \tag{4}$$

What about stability? Differentiate (4) for d to check:

$$\frac{\partial \dot{d}}{\partial d} = (1-c)(1-t)r - n \tag{5}$$

This gives rise to another stability condition. If $(1-c)(1-t)r < n$, the long-run equilibrium will be stable. Conversely, if $(1-c)(1-t)r > n$, the long-run equilibrium will be unstable. Take a numerical example with $c = 0.9$, $t = 0.2$, $n = 0.02$ and $r = 0.04$. This delivers $(1-c)(1-t)r = 0.0032$. So, from the empirical point of view, this condition seems always to be met. Therefore the long-run equilibrium will in fact be stable. In this sense, endogenous fiscal policy can sustained. Compare this to exogenous fiscal policy, where the stability condition was $(1-c)(1-t)r < [1-c(1-t)]n$. Thus endogenous fiscal policy is more likely to be stable.

In the long-run equilibrium, the motion of public debt per head comes to a standstill $\dot{d} = 0$. This together with (4) yields:

$$d = \frac{(1-c)(1-t)\bar{y} - i}{n - (1-c)(1-t)r} \tag{6}$$

Let the stability condition $(1-c)(1-t)r < n$ be fulfilled. Then a reduction in investment per head leads to an increase in public debt per head.

Now consider the consequences of a fall in investment per head in greater detail. In the short run, as a response, the government raises its purchases per head. Then, in the medium run, public debt per head starts to pile up. To counter-act this, the government period by period lowers its purchases per head.

At this point the question arises whether government purchases per head will fall below their initial level. To answer this equestion, differentiate (3) for i to get $\partial g / \partial i = -c(1-t)r\partial d / \partial i - 1$. Likewise differentiate (6) for i to get $\partial d / \partial i = -1 / [n - (1-c)(1-t)r]$. Then dispense with $\partial d/\partial i$ to achieve:

$$\frac{\partial g}{\partial i} = \frac{(1-t)r - n}{n - (1-c)(1-t)r} \tag{7}$$

Let $(1 - t)r > n$. Hence a reduction in investment per head leads to a reduction in government purchases per head. As an outcome, government purchases per head in the long run indeed fall below their initial level. The time path of government purchases per head is reminiscent of that obtained under a fixed tax per head, cf. figure 4 in section 2.2.

3.3. Wealth in Consumption Function

We postulate the consumption function $cc = c(1 - t)(y + rd) + \alpha d$, where αd stands for the wealth effect. Let fiscal policy be exogenous. The short-run equilibrium can be described by a system of two equations:

$$y = c(1-t)(y+rd) + \alpha d + i + g \tag{1}$$
$$\dot{d} = g + rd - t(y+rd) - nd \tag{2}$$

In this version $\dot{d}$ and y are endogenous. Solve equation (1) for output per head:

$$y = \frac{i + g + c(1-t)rd + \alpha d}{1 - c(1-t)} \tag{3}$$

Next we discuss stability. Differentiate (2) for d to get $\partial\dot{d}/\partial d = (1-t)r - t\partial y/\partial d - n$. Similary differentiate (3) for d to get $\partial y/\partial d = [c(1-t)r + \alpha]/[1 - c(1-t)]$. Then throw out $\partial y/\partial d$ to establish the stability condition:

$$(1-c)(1-t)r < \alpha t + (1-c+ct)n \tag{4}$$

Take a numerical example with $c = 0.9$, $t = 0.2$, $n = 0.02$, $r = 0.04$ and $\alpha = 0.01$. In this case, the stability condition will be fulfilled $0.0032 < 0.0076$. Compare this to an economy without wealth effect $\alpha = 0$, where the stability condition is $0.0032 < 0.0056$. As a result, the wealth effect increases (the likelihood of) stability.

To better understand the working of the model, have a look at a full numerical example. Let the parameter values be $c = 0.9$, $t = 0.2$, $n = 0.02$, $r = 0.04$, $i = 8$, $g = 20$ and $\alpha = 0.01$. The government raises its purchases per head from 20 to 21, thereby disrupting the long-term equilibrium. In the short term, this measure elevates output per head from 100 to 104. Then, in the intermediate term, public debt per head builds up from 0 to 18. On that account, output per head keeps on climbing from 104 to 106. Table 11 gives a synopsis. Last but not least, contrast this economy and an economy without wealth effect, focusing on the long-term equilibrium after shock. The reader may wish to refer to table 12. As a finding, the wealth effect reduces the long-term multipliers.

Table 11
Wealth in Consumption Function
Increase in Government Purchases Per Head

	1	2	3
g	20	21	21
y	100	103.6	106
d	0	0	18.2

Table 12
Increase in Government Purchases Per Head
Long-Run Effects

α	0	0.01
y	107	106
d	33.3	18.2

4. Summary

To begin with, we assume that the government fixes the deficit per head. First have a look at exogenous fiscal policy. In a growing economy, the long-run equilibrium will be stable. In a stationary economy, on the other hand, the long-run equilibrium will be unstable. Henceforth we assume a growing economy. Now suppose that the government increases its purchases per head as well as the deficit per head. In the short run, this policy measure brings up output per head. Then, in the medium run, public debt per head starts to grow. That is why the government must increase the tax per head. Output per head, however, does not move any more. Put another way, there is a one-time jump in output per head. In this sense, exogenous fiscal policy can be sustained.

Second take a glance at endogenous fiscal policy. As response to a shock, the government continuously adjusts both its purchases per head and the deficit per head so as to maintain full employment all the time. As a finding, the long-run equilibrium will be stable. In this sense, endogenous fiscal policy can be sustained.

Third catch a glimpse of investment and capital. As a result, there exists a stability condition. Regard for instance an increase in autonomous consumption per head. In the short run, the shock raises output per head and investment per head. Then, in the medium run, capital per head begins to accumulate. Owing to that, investment per head and output per head come down again. But they do not fall below their initial levels. Fourth, with capital and endogenous fiscal policy, the long-run equilibrium will be stable.

Fifth consider money finance of the budget deficit. As a consequence, the long-run equilibrium will be stable. Now let the government increase its purchases per head and the deficit per head. In the short run, this action enhances output per head. Then, in the medium run, money supply per head starts to grow. For that reason, output per head continues to rise. In this sense, money finance of the budget deficit can be sustained.

So far we assumed that the government fixes the deficit per head. Now, instead, we shall assume that the government fixes the tax per head. First have a look at exogenous fiscal policy. The analysis yields a stability condition. If the interest rate exceeds growth rate, the long-run equilibrium will be unstable. Conversely, if the interest rate falls short of the growth rate, the long-run equilibrium will be stable. Empirically speaking, the interest rate surpasses the growth rate, so the long-run equilibrium will in fact be unstable. Imagine that the government increases its purchases per head, holding the tax per head constant. In the short run, this drives up output per head. Then, in the medium run, public debt per head builds up. Due to that, output per head keeps on climbing. And what is more, in the long run, both public debt per head and output per head tend to explode. In this sense, exogenous fiscal policy cannot be sustained.

Second take a glance at endogenous fiscal policy. The government continuously adjusts its purchases per head so as to maintain full employment all the time. Here a stability condition occurs that from the empirical point of view seems to be fulfilled. Regard for instance a drop in investment per head. In the short run, to counteract this, the government increases its purchases per head. Then, in the medium run, public debt per head piles up. To compensate for this, the government reduces its purchases per head. It is worth noting that in the long run government purchases per head fall well below their initial level. In this sense, endogenous fiscal policy can be sustained.

Finally we assume that the government fixes the tax rate. First catch a glimpse of exogenous fiscal policy. This gives rise to a stability condition. For the moment let this condition be met. Now suppose that the government increases its purchases per head, holding the tax rate constant. In the short run, this boosts output per head. Then, in the medium run, public debt per head begins to accumulate. By virtue of that, output per head continues to soar. In this sense, exogenous fiscal policy can possibly be sustained.

Second consider endogenous fiscal policy. Here a stability condition exists that empirically seems to be sound. Imagine for instance a cut in investment per head. In the short run, to offset this, the government raises its purchases per head. Then, in the medium run, public debt per head starts growing. To correct for this, the government lowers its purchases per head. And in the long run, government

Table 13
Closed Economy
Stability of Long-Run Equilibrium

fixed deficit per head	
exogenous fiscal policy	stable
endogenous fiscal policy	stable
investment and capital	condition
capital and fiscal policy	stable
monetary policy	stable
money finance of budget deficit	stable
fixed tax per head	
exogenous fiscal policy	unstable
endogenous fiscal policy	stable
fixed tax rate	
exogenous fiscal policy	condition
endogenous fiscal policy	stable

purchases per head fall well below their initial level. In this sense, endogenous fiscal policy can be sustained.

To conclude, a fixed deficit per head can be sustained. A fixed tax per head, however, cannot be sustained. And a fixed tax rate can possibly be sustained. Over and above that, endogenous fiscal policy can be sustained in any case. Tables 13 and 14 present a synopsis.

Table 14
Closed Economy
Sustainability of Fiscal Policy

	exogenous fiscal policy	endogenous fiscal policy
fixed deficit per head	sustainable	sustainable
fixed tax per head	not sustainable	sustainable
fixed tax rate	condition	sustainable

PART II

OPEN ECONOMY

CHAPTER I. FIXED EXCHANGE RATE

1. Economy without Public Sector

1.1. Basic Model

The investigation will be conducted within a small open economy characterized by perfect capital mobility. For the small open economy, the foreign interest rate is given exogenously $r^* = const$. Perfect capital mobility means that the domestic interest rate coincides with the foreign interest rate $r = r^*$. Therefore the domestic interest rate will be constant, too. Without losing generality, let the exchange rate be unity.

To begin with, we shed some light on the foreign sector. Exports per head are fixed on a per capita basis $x = const$. Multiplying exports per head by labour supply gives the total of exports $X = xN$. Strictly speaking, foreign residents fix their demand for domestic goods per head of domestic labour supply. For this assumption to make sense, the growth rate of domestic labour supply must equal the growth rate of foreign labour supply. Domestic residents earn the interest r on foreign assets F, so the interest inflow amounts to rF. The income of domestic residents consists of domestic income and the interest inflow $Y + rF$. Domestic residents spend a certain fraction of their income on foreign goods $Q = q(Y + rF)$ with import rate $q = const$. The current account surplus can be defined as the excess of exports and the interest inflow over imports $Z = X + rF - Q$. The current account surplus in turn adds to foreign assets $\dot{F} = Z$. Putting all building blocks together, we arrive to $\dot{F} = xN + rF - q(Y + rF)$.

Next a few words will be said on the goods market. Households consume a specified proportion of their income $C = c(Y + rF)$ with $c = const$. Let the import rate be less than the consumption rate $q < c$. Firms fix investment on a per capita basis $I = iN$ with $i = const$. Domestic output is controlled by the demand for domestic goods $Y = C + I + X - Q$. From this one can deduce $Y = (c - q)(Y + rF) + iN + xN$.

Relying on this groundwork, the short-run equilibrium can be represented by a system of three equations:

$$Y = (c-q)(Y+rF)+iN+xN \tag{1}$$

$$\dot{F} = xN+rF-q(Y+rF) \tag{2}$$

$$\dot{N} = nN \tag{3}$$

Here $\dot{F}$, $\dot{N}$ and Y are endogenous.

It proves useful to carry out the analysis in per capita terms. $y = Y/N$ denotes domestic income per head, and $f = F/N$ is foreign assets per head. Accordingly equation (1) can be restated as $y = (c - q)(y + rf) + i + x$. Now take the time derivative of foreign assets per head $\dot{f} = \dot{F}/N - F\dot{N}/N^2$. Then substitute equations (2) and (3) to reach $\dot{f} = x + rf - q(y + rf) - nf$. Hence the short-run equilibrium in per capita terms can be captured by a system of two equations:

$$y = (c-q)(y+rf)+i+x \tag{4}$$

$$\dot{f} = x+rf-q(y+rf)-nf \tag{5}$$

In this version $\dot{f}$ and y are endogenous.

What are the main properties of the short-run equilibrium? To answer this question, solve equation (4) for domestic output per head:

$$y = \frac{i+x+(c-q)rf}{1-c+q} \tag{6}$$

Obviously, an increase in exports per head causes an increase in domestic output per head. The same applies to an increase in investment per head (or, for that matter, in foreign assets per head). Initially, let the foreign position be balanced $f = 0$. Then an increase in the consumption rate causes an increase in domestic output per head. An increase in the import rate, the other way round, causes a reduction in domestic output per head.

The short-run equilibrium can be further compressed to a single differential equation $\dot{f} = \varepsilon(f)$. Eliminate $y + rf$ in equation (5) by means of equation (4) and rearrange:

$$\dot{f} = \frac{(1-c)(x+rf)-qi}{1-c+q} - nf \tag{7}$$

With the help of (7), we can probe into stability. Differentiate (7) for f:

$$\frac{\partial \dot{f}}{\partial f} = \frac{(1-c)r}{1-c+q} - n \tag{8}$$

This gives rise to a stability condition:

$$(1-c)r < (1-c+q)n \tag{9}$$

Consider a numerical example with $c = 0.9$, $q = 0.3$, $n = 0.02$ and $r = 0.04$. This yields $(1 - c)r = 0.004 < (1 - c + q)n = 0.008$. In this case, the long-run equilibrium will be stable. Moreover, there exists a critical level of the consumption rate $c' = 0.7$. If the consumption rate exceeds 0.7, the long-run equilibrium will be stable. Conversely, if the consumption rate falls short of 0.7, the long-run equilibrium will be unstable. Generally speaking, if the growth rate is high, the long-run equilibrium will be stable. However, if the foreign interest rate is high, the long-run equilibrium will be unstable. If the consumption rate is high, we will be back at stability. And the same holds for a high import rate. From this time on, let the stability condition be fulfilled.

In the long-run equilibrium, foreign assets per head stop to adjust $\dot{f} = 0$. Combine this with equation (7) to accomplish:

$$f = \frac{(1-c)x-qi}{(1-c+q)n-(1-c)r} \tag{10}$$

f will be positive if and only if $(1 - c)x > qi$. If exports per head are high, then foreign assets per head will be positive. But if investment per head is high, then foreign assets per head will be negative. The same is true for a high consumption rate (or for a high import rate).

Put another way, the high-exporting country will be a creditor, while the low-exporting country will be a debtor. On the other hand, the high-investing country will be a debtor, while the low-investing country will be a creditor. Similarly, the high-consuming country will be a debtor, whereas the low-consuming country will be a creditor. What is equivalent, the high-saving country will be a creditor, whereas the low-saving country will be a debtor. The high-importing country will be a debtor, yet the low-importing country will be creditor. A high interest rate implies low investment per head, so foreign assets per head will be positive. In this sense, when the foreign interest rate is high, the country in question will be a creditor. The other way round, when the foreign interest is low, the country will be a debtor. Be careful, in a two-country model this might be different.

Beyond that, an increase in exports per head leads to an increase in foreign assets per head. However, an increase in investment per head leads to a decline in foreign assets per head. Let the country be a creditor. Then an increase in the growth rate reduces foreign assets per head. Conversely, let the country be a debtor. Then an increase in the growth rate reduces foreign debt per head.

Now have a look at the dynamics of output per head. First regard an increase in exports per head. In the short run, the shock enhances output per head. Then, in the medium run, foreign assets per head start to grow. On those grounds, output per head continues to rise. Correspondingly, figure 1 reveals the time path of output per head.

Second imagine an increase in investment per head. In the short run, this raises output per head. Then, in the medium run, foreign assets per head start to decline, thereby gradually lowering output per head. Here the question comes up whether output per head will fall below its initial level. To solve this problem, differentiate equation (6) for i, paying heed to equation (10). As a corollary, the necessary and sufficient condition for $\partial y/\partial i$ to be negative is:

$$(1-c)r + (c-q)qr > (1-c+q)n \tag{11}$$

Compare this with the stability condition in (9) to realize that stability does not involve $\partial y/\partial i < 0$.

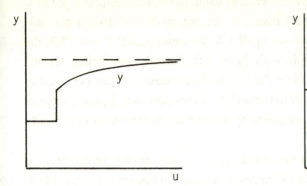

Figure 1
Increase in Exports Per Head

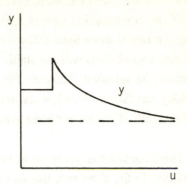

Figure 2
Increase in Investment Per Head

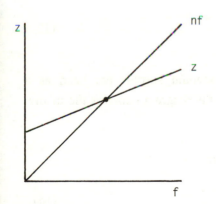

Figure 3
Current Account Surplus Per Head

In the numerical example given above, the condition for $\partial y/\partial i < 0$ is met $0.0112 > 0.008$. Besides, there exists a critical value of the consumption rate $c'' = 1.3$. If the consumption rate is less than 1.3, we get $\partial y/\partial i < 0$. But if the consumption rate is more than 1.3, we get $\partial y/\partial i > 0$. To sum up, if $0.7 < c < 1.3$, the long-run equilibrium will be stable with $\partial y/\partial i < 0$. For the time being, let this condition be satisfied. Thus we have $\partial y/\partial i < 0$. That means, output per head in the long run falls well below its initial level. As a consequence, figure 2 depicts the time path of output per head generated by an increase in investment per head.

Third consider an increase in the growth rate. Let the country in question be a creditor. In the short run, the shock leaves no impact on output per head. Then, in the medium run, foreign assets per head begin to decumulate. Owing to that, output per head comes down slowly. The other way round, let the country be a debtor. In the short run, again, the shock has no influence on output per head. Then, in the medium run, foreign debt per head begins to decumulate. Due to that, output per head goes up period by period.

Next we shall examine the current account in greater detail. In the short-run equilibrium we have $\dot{F} = Z$. This can be expressed in per capita terms as $\dot{f} = z - nf$, where z is the current account surplus per head. Compare this to equation (7) to verify:

$$z = \frac{(1-c)(x+rf) - qi}{1-c+q} \tag{12}$$

Correspondingly figure 3 shows the current account surplus per head as a function of foreign assets per head. In addition the diagram contains the nf ray. And stability implies $\partial z/\partial i < n$.

In the long-run equilibrium it comes true that:

$$z = nf \tag{13}$$

In the diagram, the long-run equilibrium is marked by the point of intersection. If exports per head are high, then foreign assets per head will be positive, so the current account surplus per head will be positive, too. In other words, the high-exporting country will run a current account surplus. But if investment per head

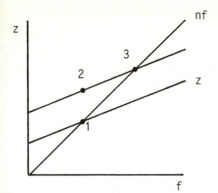

Figure 4
Increase in Exports Per Head

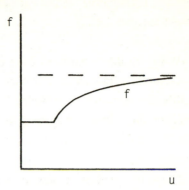

Figure 5
Increase in Exports Per Head

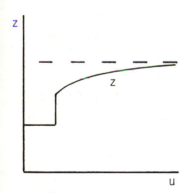

Figure 6
Increase in Exports Per Head

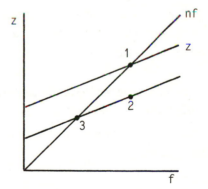

Figure 7
Increase in Investment Per Head

is high, then foreign assets per head will be negative, so the current account surplus will be negative, too. That is to say, the high-investing country will run a current account deficit.

What are the dynamics of the current account surplus per head? First consider an increase in exports per head. Initially, let the economy be in the long-run equilibrium, see point 1 in figure 4. Then exports per head go up. In the diagram, therefore, the z line shifts upwards. The short-run equilibrium after shock lies in point 2, and the long-run equilibrium after shock lies in point 3.

Properly speaking, z denotes the actual current account surplus per head. As opposed to that, nf is the current account surplus per head that is required to keep foreign assets per head constant. In the short run, the current account surplus per head exceeds the required level, thus foreign assets per head will grow. Figure 5 plots the associated time path of foreign assets per head, and figure 6 graphs the trajectory of the current account surplus per head. In the short run, the current account surplus per head jumps up. Then, in the medium run, it continues to rise.

Second regard an increase in investment per head. In figure 7, the z line shifts downwards. In the short term, the current account surplus per head falls short of the required level, hence foreign assets per head will decline. Figure 8 exhibits the accompanying time path of foreign assets per head, and figure 9 indicates how the current account surplus per head travels through time. In the short term, the current account surplus per head drops. Then, in the intermediate term, it continues to fall.

At this stage we leave the current account and turn to the trade account. Let h be the trade surplus per head. The current account surplus is the sum of the trade surplus and the interest inflow, in per capita terms, respectively $z = h + rf$. From this follows:

$$h = z - rf \tag{14}$$

Take glance at the short-run effects. An increase in exports per head causes an increase in the current account surplus per head and, thus, in the trade surplus per head. Yet an increase in investment per head causes a reduction in the current account surplus per head and, hence, in the trade surplus per head. An increase in

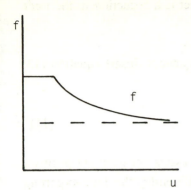

Figure 8

Increase in Investment Per Head

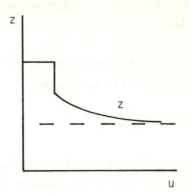

Figure 9

Increase in Investment Per Head

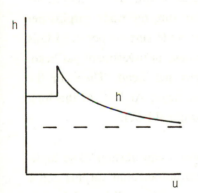

Figure 10

Increase in Exports Per Head

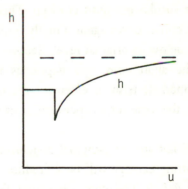

Figure 11

Increase in Investment Per Head

foreign assets per head causes an increase in both the current account surplus per head and the interest inflow per head. The net effect is a reduction in the trade surplus per head.

Further, catch a glimpse of the long-run consequences. Insert equation (13) into equation (14) and rearrange:

$$h = -(r - n)f \qquad (15)$$

Let $r > n$. If exports per head are high, then foreign assets per head are positive, so the trade surplus per head is negative. Put differently, the high-exporting country will run a trade deficit, which at first sight seems to be a bit paradoxical. Conversely, if investment per head is high, then foreign assets per head are negative, so the trade surplus per head is positive. Put another way, the high-investing country will run a trade surplus. What is more, an increase in exports per head raises foreign assets per head and lowers the trade surplus per head (in mathematical terms). An increase in investment per head, on the other hand, lowers foreign assets per head and raises the trade surplus per head.

Figures 10 and 11 display the time paths of the trade surplus per head, generated by an increase in exports per head or investment per head, respectively. First imagine an increase in exports per head. In the short run, as a reaction, the trade surplus per head goes up. Then, in the medium run, the trade surplus per head comes down again. Finally, in the long run, the trade surplus per head falls well below its original level. Second think of an increase in investment per head. In the short term, this depresses the trade surplus per head. Then, in the intermediate term, it enhances the trade surplus per head. At last, in the long term, the trade surplus per head rises well above its original level.

What are the principal conclusions for the long-run equilibrium? The high-exporting country will be a creditor. It will run a current account surplus and a trade deficit. The other way round, the high-investing country will be a debtor. It will run a current account deficit and a trade surplus.

Coming to an end, we shall trace out the full process of adjustment in a coherent way, putting special emphasis on the chain of cause and effect. First take an increase in exports per head. At the beginning, the economy is in the long-run equilibrium. Let the trade account, the current account and the foreign position be balanced. Output per head does not move. Against this background, exports per head spring up. In the short run, this raises output per head. Both the trade account and the current account get into surplus.

In the medium run, the current account surplus per head contributes to the accumulation of foreign assets per head. The ensuing growth of the interest inflow enlarges the income of domestic residents, their consumption and hence output, in per capita terms, respectively. Moreover, the growth of the interest inflow per head augments the current account surplus per head. Besides, the growth of the income of domestic residents per head brings up imports per head, thus cutting back the trade surplus per head. After some time, the trade surplus changes into a trade deficit.

Asymptotically, the economy converges to a new long-run equilibrium. The trade deficit per head, the current account surplus per head and foreign assets per head are constant. Output per head does not move any more. To sum up, the country will be a creditor. It registers a current account surplus and a trade deficit. For the time paths see figures 1, 4, 5, 6 and 10.

Second take an increase in investment per head. Initially the economy is in the steady state. Let the trade account, the current account and the foreign position be balanced. Output per head is uniform. In this situation, investment per head jumps up. In the short term, this enhances output per head. Due to the rise in imports per head, both the trade account and the current account get into deficit.

In the intermediate term, the current account deficit per head contributes to the accumulation of foreign debt per head. The subsequent expansion of the interest outflow reduces the income of domestic residents, their consumption and hence output, in per capita terms, respectively. Further, the expansion of the interest outflow per head augments the current account deficit per head. Beyond that, the contraction of the income of domestic residents per head diminishes imports per head and, thus, the trade deficit per head. After some time, the trade deficit turns into a trade surplus.

In the new steady state, the trade surplus per head, the current account deficit per head and foreign debt per head stop adjusting. Output per head is again uniform. To conclude, the country will be a debtor. It experiences a current account deficit and a trade surplus. For the time paths see figures 2, 7, 8, 9 and 11.

In summary, the analysis gives rise to a stability condition that from the empirical point of view will be fulfilled. First consider an increase in exports per head. In the short run, this lifts output per head. Then, in the medium run, foreign assets per head start to accumulate. That is why output per head keeps on climbing. Second regard an increase in investment per head. In the short run, this drives up output per head. Then, in the medium run, foreign assets per head begin to decumulate. Owing to that, output per head comes down again. It is worth stressing that, in the long run, output per head falls well below its initial level. In this sense, a fixed exchange rate can be sustained.

1.2. Numerical Example

To illustrate the basic model, we shall consider a numerical example. In doing this, we shall proceed in two steps. To begin with, we shall regard an export shock. Then we shall address an investment shock. Let the parameter values be $c = 0.9$, $q = 0.3$, $n = 0.02$, $r = 0.04$, $i = 10$ and $x = 30$. Initially the economy is in the long-run equilibrium. According to equation (10) from section 1.1. the foreign position is balanced $f = 0$. And according to equation (6) output per head is 100. Of course, the parameter values have been chosen in such a way as to produce these results.

Under these circumstances the economy is hit by a shock, exports per head go up from 30 to 31. In the short run, output per head rises from 100 to 102.5. Then, in the medium run, foreign assets per head come into existence, building up slowly from 0 to 25. Therefore output per head continues to rise from 102.5 to 104. As a finding, the short-run multiplier is 2.5, and the long-run multiplier is 4.

The income of domestic residents per head $y + rf$ in the short run jumps up from 100 to 102.5. Then, in the medium run, it climbs from 102.5 up to 105. The current account surplus per head in the short run springs up from 0 to 0.25. Then, in the medium run, it climbs from 0.25 up to 0.5. The trade surplus per head in the short run rises quickly from 0 to 0.25. Then, in the medium run, it falls slowly from 0.25 down to − 0.5. And the foreign asset ratio f/y in the medium run goes up from 0 to 0.24. Table 15 presents an overview of this process. Column 1 gives the pre-shock steady state, column 2 the short-run equilibrium after shock, and column 3 the post-shock steady state.

Table 15
Fixed Exchange Rate
Increase in Exports Per Head

	1	2	3
x	30	31	31
f	0	0	25
y	100	102.5	104
y+rf	100	102.5	105
z	0	0.25	0.5
h	0	0.25	− 0.5
f/y	0	0	0.24

Here a comment is in place concerning the speed of adjustment. The half-life of this process is 69 years. That is, in period 69 foreign assets per head are 12.46. So this is a very slow process.

At this juncture we leave the export shock and turn to the investment shock. At the start the economy is in the long-term equilibrium, with exports per head being back at 30. Then investment per head increases from 10 to 11. In the short term, this raises output per head from 100 to 102.5. Then, in the intermediate term, foreign debt per head emerges, piling up slowly from 0 to 75. This in turn lowers output per head from 102.5 to 98, round by round. As a byproduct, the short-term multiplier is + 2.5, whereas the long-term multiplier is − 2.

The income per head of domestic residents y + rf in the short term mounts from 100 to 102.5. Then, in the intermediate term, it descends from 102.5 to 95. The current account deficit per head in the short term climbs from 0 to 0.8. Then, in the intermediate term, it keeps on climbing until it reaches 1.5. The trade deficit per head in the short term rises from 0 to 0.8. Then, in the intermediate term, it falls from 0.8 down to − 1.5. And the foreign debt ratio (− f/y) expands from 0 to 0.77. Table 16 offers a synopsis of this process.

Table 16
Fixed Exchange Rate
Increase in Investment Per Head

	1	2	3
i	10	11	11
f	0	0	− 75
y	100	102.5	98
y+rf	100	102.5	95
z	0	− 0.8	− 1.5
h	0	− 0.8	1.5
f/y	0	0	− 0.77

1.3. Wealth in Consumption Function

In this section we introduce wealth into the consumption function $cc = c(y + rf) + c\alpha f$ as well as the import function $qq = q(y + rf) + q\alpha f$. Let be $\alpha > 0$. Think of a unit increase in foreign assets per head. Then the wealth effect on consumption per head is $c\alpha$. Correspondingly, the wealth effect on imports per head is $q\alpha$. Along the same lines as in section 1.1. the temporary equilibrium can be caught by a system of two equations:

$$y = (c - q)(y + rf + \alpha f) + i + x \tag{1}$$

$$\dot{f} = x + rf - q(y + rf + \alpha f) - nf \tag{2}$$

Here $\dot{f}$ and y are endogenous. Now state output per head explicitly:

$$y = \frac{i + x + (c - q)(\alpha + r)f}{1 - c + q} \tag{3}$$

The temporary equilibrium can be reformulated as a single differential equation $\dot{f} = \varepsilon(f)$. Get rid of $y + rf + \alpha f$ in (2) by making use of (1) and reshuffle terms:

$$\dot{f} = \frac{(1 - c)(x + rf) - q(i + \alpha f)}{1 - c + q} - nf \tag{4}$$

On this basis we can inquire into stability. Differentiate (4) for f to accomplish:

$$\frac{\partial \dot{f}}{\partial f} = \frac{(1 - c)r - q\alpha}{1 - c + q} - n \tag{5}$$

The evaluation of (5) delivers a stability condition:

$$(1 - c)r < (1 - c + q)n + \alpha q \tag{6}$$

Apparently an increase in α occasions an increase in (the likelihood of) stability.

To see this more clearly, take a numerical example with c = 0.9, q = 0.3, n = 0.02, r = 0.04 and α = 0.01. In this case we have $(1 - c)r = 0.004 < (1 - c + q)n + \alpha q = 0.011$. From the empirical point of view, this condition seems to be sound. As a consequence, the permanent equilibrium will indeed be stable. Over and above that, there exists a critical level of the marginal propensity to consume c' = 0.55. When the propensity to consume is larger than 0.55, the permanent equilibrium will be stable. On the other hand, when the propensity to consume is smaller than 0.55, the permanent equilibrium will be unstable.

Finally we establish the permanent equilibrium. In the long run, foreign assets per head are invariant $\dot{f} = 0$. This together with (4) provides:

$$f = \frac{(1-c)x - qi}{(1-c+q)n + \alpha q - (1-c)r} \tag{7}$$

Table 17 throws some more light on the long-run effects in the numerical example. As an outcome, wealth in the consumption function definitely reduces all of the long-run multipliers. This holds irrespective of the source of disturbance. And this applies to foreign assets per head as well as to output per head.

Table 17
Wealth in Consumption Function
Long-Run Multipliers

α	0.01	0
$\partial f / \partial x$	14.3	25
$\partial y / \partial x$	3.6	2
$\partial f / \partial i$	− 42.9	− 75
$\partial y / \partial i$	− 0.7	− 2

1.4. Imperfect Capital Mobility

In the current section we assume that the growth of foreign debt per head leads to credit rationing. Here δ symbolizes foreign debt per head. The short-run equilibrium of output per head is (cf. equation (6) from section 1.1.):

$$y = \frac{i + x - (c - q)r\delta}{1 - c + q} \qquad (1)$$

Consider for instance a reduction in exports per head. In the short run, this lowers output per head. Then, in the medium run, foreign debt per head starts to accumulate. Therefore output per head continues to fall.

As soon as foreign debt per head reaches a critical level, the constraint becomes operative. Here μ stands for the maximum feasible value of foreign debt per head. The short-run equilibrium of output per head subject to the constraint $\delta = \mu$ is:

$$y = \frac{i + x - (c - q)r\mu}{1 - c + q} \qquad (2)$$

As an implication, output per head will be constant. Figures 1 and 2 elucidate the pertinent time paths. In figure 1, foreign debt per head grows until it hits the ceiling given by μ. In figure 2, as a consequence, output per head declines until it hits the floor given by equation (2) and marked by the arrow in the picture.

The current account deficit per head is (cf. equation (5) in section 1.1.) $\gamma = q(y - r\delta) + r\delta - x$. Now dispense with y and δ to find out the current account deficit per head that will hold under credit rationing:

$$\gamma = \frac{qi - (1 - c)(x - r\mu)}{1 - c + q} \qquad (3)$$

Of course, the capital inflow per head will be constrained, too, $n\delta = n\mu$. As an important conclusion, the capital inflow will not be sufficient to finance the cur-

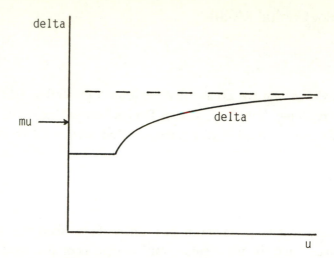

Figure 1
Foreign Debt Per Head

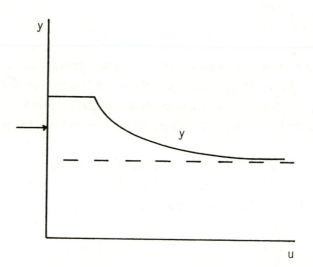

Figure 2
Output Per Head

rent account deficit. These difficulties can only be overcome by intervening in the foreign exchange market or by devaluing domestic currency.

1.5. Devaluation

Foreign assets can be denominated either in domestic currency or in foreign currency. At first we shall give a rough outline of denomination in domestic currency. Then we shall study denomination in foreign currency in greater detail. Let us begin with foreign assets denominated in domestic currency. e denotes the nominal exchange rate. p is the price of domestic goods, expressed in domestic currency. Similarly p* is the price of foreign goods, expressed in foreign currency. So ep*/p is the real exchange rate. f is foreign assets per head denominated in domestic currency. Hence f/p is foreign assets per head expressed in domestic goods. x is exports per head expressed in domestic goods. Exports per head are an increasing function of the real exchange rate x = jep*/p with sensitivity j = const. For ease of exposition let be p = p* = 1. Thus f can be interpreted as foreign assets per head expressed in domestic goods. Likewise rf can be viewed as the interest inflow per head expressed in domestic goods. x = je is exports per head stated in domestic goods. And q(y + rf) is imports per head in terms of domestic goods.

In full analogy to section 1.1. the short-run equilibrium can be written as a system of two equations:

$$y = (c-q)(y+rf)+i+je \tag{1}$$

$$\dot{f} = je+rf-q(y+rf)-nf \tag{2}$$

Here $\dot{f}$ and y are endogenous. Now solve equation (1) for output per head:

$$y = \frac{i+je+(c-q)rf}{1-c+q} \tag{3}$$

From this it is evident that a devaluation (i.e. an increase in the exchange rate) brings up output per head. The model can be condensed to a first-order differential equation:

$$\dot{f} = \frac{(1-c)(je+rf)-qi}{1-c+q} - nf \tag{4}$$

The long-run equilibrium of foreign assets per head is:

$$f = \frac{(1-c)je-qi}{(1-c+q)n-(1-c)r} \tag{5}$$

If the exchange rate is high, then foreign assets per head will be positive. Conversely, if the exchange rate is low, then foreign assets per head will be negative. That means, the country having an undervalued currency will be a creditor, other things being equal. And the country having an overvalued currency will be a debtor. What is more, a devaluation increases foreign assets per head.

Last but not least take a closer look at the dynamic effects of a devaluation. In the short run, this measure raises output per head. Then, in the medium run, foreign assets per head pile up. That is why output per head keeps on rising.

So far we supposed that foreign assets are denominated in domestic currency. Now, instead, we shall postulate that foreign assets are denominated in foreign currency. What difference does this make? Properly speaking, f symbolizes foreign assets per head denominated in foreign currency. Thus ef is foreign assets per head expressed in domestic currency. And ef/p is foreign assets per head expressed in domestic goods. To simplify matters let be $p = p^* = 1$. Then ef can be interpreted as foreign assets per head expressed in domestic goods. erf is the interest inflow per head expressed in domestic goods. $e\dot{f}$ is the change in foreign assets per head expressed in domestic goods. $x = je$ is exports per head stated in domestic goods. And $q(y + rf)$ is imports per head in terms of domestic goods.

The short-run equilibrium can be described by a system of two equations:

$$y = (c-q)(y+erf)+i+je \tag{6}$$

$$e\dot{f} = je + erf - q(y + erf) - enf \tag{7}$$

In this version $\dot{f}$ and y are endogenous. Equation (6) yields output per head:

$$y = \frac{i + je + (c - q)erf}{1 - c + q} \tag{8}$$

How does a devaluation affect output per head? To answer this question, differentiate equation (8) for e. Here a critical level of foreign assets per head emerges:

$$f' = -\frac{j}{(c - q)r} < 0 \tag{9}$$

If foreign assets per head exceed the critical level, then the devaluation increases output per head. However, if foreign assets per head fall short of the critical level, then the devaluation reduces output per head. The underlying reason is that erf goes up as e goes up. That is to say, the devaluation increases the interest outflow in terms of domestic currency, thereby reducing consumption. In judging this, we have to keep in mind that the critical level of foreign assets per head is highly negative. Therefore, as a rule, foreign assets per head will surpass the critical level. So, in the normal case, the devaluation will increase output per head.

The model can be further compressed to a single differential equation $\dot{f} = \varepsilon(f)$. Solve equation (6) for y + erf and substitute the resulting term into equation (7):

$$\dot{f} = \frac{(1 - c)(j + rf) - qi/e}{1 - c + q} - nf \tag{10}$$

What about stability? Differentiate equation (10) for f to realize:

$$\frac{\partial \dot{f}}{\partial f} = \frac{(1 - c)r}{1 - c + q} - n \tag{11}$$

This gives rise to a stability condition:

112

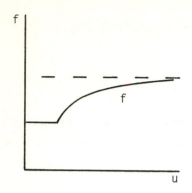

Figure 1
Foreign Assets Per Head
(in Foreign Currency)

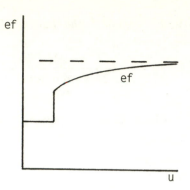

Figure 2
Foreign Assets Per Head
(in Domestic Currency)

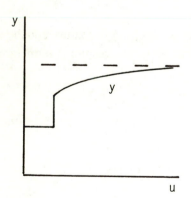

Figure 3
Output Per Head

$$(1-c)r < (1-c+q)n \tag{12}$$

Now (12) is identical to the stability condition for the standard case e = 1, cf. (9) in section 1.1.

In the long-run equilibrium the motion of foreign assets per head comes to a standstill $\dot{f} = 0$. Combine this with (10) and regroup:

$$f = \frac{(1-c)j - qi/e}{(1-c+q)n - (1-c)r} \tag{13}$$

As a consequence, a devaluation increases foreign assets per head. Figures 1 and 2 illuminate the accompanying time paths. Initially let foreign assets per head be positive. Then foreign assets per head in terms of foreign currency accumulate step by step, see figure 1. As regards foreign assets per head in terms of domestic currency, the trajectory is a little more complicated. In the short run, the devaluation induces an upward jump in foreign assets per head. Then, in the medium run, foreign assets per head keep on growing, see figure 2.

Coming to an end, we shall present the dynamic effects of a devaluation in a more coherent way. In the short run, let output per head rise. Then, in the medium run, foreign assets per head (in terms of foreign currency) build up. Thus output per head continues to rise. Figure 3 visualizes how output per head evolves over time.

1.6. Endogenous Exchange Rate Policy

In the preceding sections we assumed that exchange rate policy is exogenous. In the current section, instead, we shall assume that exchange rate policy is endogenous. More precisely, suppose that the government continuously adjusts the exchange rate so as to maintain full employment all the time. Of course, this is distinct from a regime of flexible exchange rates, cf. chapter II. In doing the analysis we posit that exchange rate expectations are static. Foreign assets can be denominated either in domestic currency or in foreign currency.

1) Denomination in domestic currency. The short-run equilibrium can be encapsulated in a system of two equations:

$$\bar{y} = (c-q)(\bar{y}+rf) + i + x + je \tag{1}$$

$$\dot{f} = x + je + rf - q(\bar{y}+rf) - nf \tag{2}$$

Here e and $\dot{f}$ are endogenous. From equation (1) one can derive the exchange rate:

$$je = \bar{y} - (c-q)(\bar{y}+rf) - i - x \tag{3}$$

Obviously a reduction in exports per head calls for a devaluation. Much the same applies to a reduction in investment per head. And an increase in foreign assets per head calls for a revaluation.

The model can be reformulated as a first-order differential equation. Get rid of je in equation (2) with the help of equation (3):

$$\dot{f} = (1-c)(\bar{y}+rf) - i - nf \tag{4}$$

On this basis we can discuss stability. Differentiate equation (4) for f:

$$\frac{\partial \dot{f}}{\partial f} = (1-c)r - n \tag{5}$$

This yields a stability condition:

$$(1-c)r < n \tag{6}$$

Empirically speaking this condition seems to be sound. Henceforth, let the condition be fulfilled.

In the long-run equilibrium, the motion of foreign assets per head comes to a halt $\dot{f} = 0$. This together with (4) provides the long-run equilibrium of foreign assets per head:

$$f = \frac{(1-c)\bar{y}-i}{n-(1-c)r} \tag{7}$$

A reduction in exports per head has no effect on foreign assets per head. But a reduction in investment per head leads to an increase in foreign assets per head.

Finally take a closer look at dynamics. First consider a reduction in exports per head. In the short run, this calls for a devaluation. Then, in the medium run, foreign assets per head do not change. Thus there is no further need for exchange rate policy. Second regard a reduction in investment per head. In the short run, this calls for a devaluation. Then, in the medium run, foreign assets per head start to grow. To counteract this, a revaluation is called for. To sum up, in the short run, the exchange rate goes up. Then, in the medium run, the exchange rate comes down again. Here the question arises whether the exchange rate in the long run falls below its original level.

To solve this problem, differentiate (3) for i, paying attention to (7). Without loss of generality, let be $j = 1$:

$$\frac{\partial e}{\partial i} = \frac{(1-q)r-n}{n-(1-c)r} \tag{8}$$

From the empirical point of view, it is rather safe to postulate $(1 - q)r > n$. On this premise we reach $\partial e / \partial i > 0$. That is to say, a reduction in investment per head calls for a reduction in the exchange rate. As a result, the exchange rate in the long run falls well below its original level. Figure 1 portrays the time path of the exchange rate. This path is clearly reflected in the trajectory of exports per head, see figure 2.

2) Denomination in foreign currency. The short-term equilibrium can be caught by a system of two equations:

$$\bar{y} = (c-q)(\bar{y}+erf)+i+je \tag{9}$$

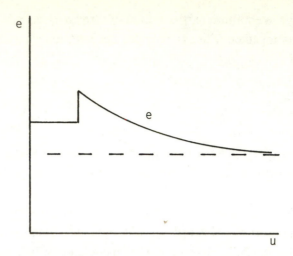

Figure 1
Endogenous Exchange Rate Policy

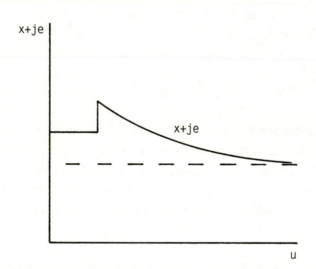

Figure 2
Export Per Head

$$e\dot{f} = je + erf - q(\bar{y} + erf) - enf \tag{10}$$

In this version e and $\dot{f}$ are endogenous. Equation (9) gives the required level of the exchange rate:

$$e = \frac{(1-c+q)\bar{y}-i}{j+(c-q)rf} \tag{11}$$

A reduction in exports per head calls for a devaluation. The same holds for a reduction in investment per head. And an increase in foreign assets per head calls for a revaluation. The model can be condensed to a single differential equation. Dispense with je in (10) by making use of (9) to accomplish:

$$e\dot{f} = (1-c)(\bar{y}+erf) - i - enf \tag{12}$$

In the long-term equilibrium, foreign assets per head stop to adjust $e\dot{f} = 0$. Join this with (12) to ascertain the long-term equilibrium of foreign assets per head (expressed in domestic currency):

$$ef = \frac{(1-c)\bar{y}-i}{n-(1-c)r} \tag{13}$$

Let be $(1-c)r < n$. Then a reduction in exports per head leaves no impact on foreign assets per head. And a reduction in investment per head leads to an increase in foreign assets per head. Incidentally, if $i = (1-c)\bar{y}$, then the foreign position will be balanced $ef = 0$.

Next we shall address stability. Solve (12) for $\dot{f}$ and eliminate e by means of (11):

$$\dot{f} = \frac{[(1-c)\bar{y}-i][j+(c-q)rf]}{(1-c+q)\bar{y}-i} + (1-c)rf - nf \tag{14}$$

Differentiate (14) for f. Here three cases can occur. First, let the initial value be $i = (1-c)\bar{y}$. That is, let be $ef = 0$. In this case there exists a stability condition:

$$(1-c)r < n \tag{15}$$

Empirically speaking this condition will be met. Second, let the initial value be $i > (1-c)\bar{y}$. That is, let be ef < 0. In this case, $(1 - c)r < n$ is sufficient for stability. And third, let the initial value be $i < (1-c)\bar{y}$. That is, let be ef > 0. In this case, if $[(1-c)\bar{y}-i]/[(1-c+q)\bar{y}-i]$ is small, then the long-term equilibrium will be stable.

In summary, the analysis gives rise to a stability condition that from the empirical point of view seems to be sound. First imagine a reduction in exports per head. In the short run, this calls for a devaluation. Then, in the medium run, foreign assets per head do not respond. That is why no further action is needed. Second imagine a reduction in investment per head. In the short run, this calls for a devaluation. Then, in the medium run, foreign assets per head begin to accumulate. This in turn calls for a revaluation. In the long run, the exchange rate will fall below its original level. In this sense, endogenous exchange rate policy can be sustained.

1.7. Full Model

First have a look at the portfolio of the private sector. Without losing generality, let the exchange rate be unity. a_1 denotes assets per head held by the private sector. m_1 is money per head, b_1 is domestic bonds per head, and f_1 is foreign bonds per head, held by the private sector, respectively. The wealth identity of the private sector is $a_1 = m_1 + b_1 + f_1$.

Second take a glance at the portfolio of the central bank. a_2 symbolizes assets per head held by the central bank, b_2 is domestic bonds per head held by the central bank, and f_2 is foreign bonds per head held by the central bank. Accordingly, the wealth identity of the monetary authority is $a_2 = b_2 + f_2$. Moreover, the balance sheet equation of the central bank is $b_2 + f_2 = m_1$.

The central bank earns the interest rate r on its assets $b_2 + f_2$. We assume that the interest earnings of the central bank $r(b_2 + f_2)$ are distributed to the private sector. On these grounds the income of domestic residents amounts to $y - rb_2 + rf_1 + r(b_2 + f_2) = y + rf_1 + rf_2$.

Third catch a glimpse of the money market. Money demand is an increasing function of the income of domestic residents, in per capita terms respectively, and a decreasing function of the interest rate $\kappa(y + rf_1 + rf_2) - \delta r$. Here $\kappa > 0$ stands for income sensitivity, and $\delta > 0$ for interest sensitivity. In what follows, δr can be suppressed, by virtue of the assumption that r is constant. Further m_1 denotes money supply per head. And the money market clears $m_1 = \kappa(y + rf_1 + rf_2)$.

Resting on this foundation, the short-run equilibrium can be enshrined in a system of six equations:

$$y = (c - q)(y + rf_1 + rf_2) + i + x \tag{1}$$

$$m_1 = \kappa(y + rf_1 + rf_2) \tag{2}$$

$$b_2 + f_2 = m_1 \tag{3}$$

$$a_1 = m_1 + b_1 + f_1 \tag{4}$$

$$s = (1 - c)(y + rf_1 + rf_2) \tag{5}$$

$$\dot{a}_1 = s - na_1 \tag{6}$$

In this version $\dot{a}_1$, f_1, f_2, m_1, s and y are endogenous. Equation (1) is the goods market equation, (2) is the money market equation, (3) is the balance sheet equation, and (4) is the wealth identity. Equation (5) is the savings function with savings per head s. And equation (6) has it that savings add to the stock of assets. Equation (1) gives y, (2) gives m_1, (3) gives f_2, (4) gives f_1, (5) gives s, and (6) gives $\dot{a}_1$.

Now amalgamate equations (3) and (4) to find $a_1 = b_1 + b_2 + f_1 + f_2$. Let $b = b_1 + b_2$ be the total of domestic bonds, and let $f = f_1 + f_2$ be the total of foreign bonds. This yields $a_1 = b + f$. In addition, substitute $a_1 = b + f$ as well as (4) into (6) to realize $\dot{b} + \dot{f} = (1 - c)(y + rf) - nb - nf$. Domestic bonds are issued in order to finance domestic investment $\dot{b} = i - nb$. For ease of exposition, let be $i = nb$, which implies $\dot{b} = 0$. In this way we arrive at $\dot{f} = (1-c)(y+rf) - i - nf$.

Therefore the model can be compressed to a system of two equations:

$$y = (c-q)(y+rf) + i + x \tag{7}$$

$$\dot{f} = (1-c)(y+rf) - i - nf \tag{8}$$

Here $\dot{f}$ and y are endogenous. As an important result, this is identical to the basic model, cf. section 1.1. It is also worth noting that f includes both foreign bonds held by the private sector and foreign bonds held by the central bank.

Next we shall keep track of the process of adjustment induced by a (favourable) export shock. At the beginning, the economy is in the long-run equilibrium. The current account surplus per head is uniform. The same applies to foreign bonds per head held by the private sector, to foreign bonds per head held by the central bank, to money per head held by the private sector, as well as to output per head. In the steady state, domestic residents buy money from the central bank, paying for it by foreign bonds.

In this situation, exports per head go up. In the short run, this raises output per head and thus money demand per head. That means, domestic residents buy some extra money from the central bank, paying for it by foreign bonds again. Money per head held by the private sector rises, foreign bonds per head held by the private sector fall, and foreign bonds held by the central bank rise. Strictly speaking it holds $\Delta f_2 = -\Delta f_1 = \Delta m_1$. Besides, the increase in exports per head brings about an increase in the current account surplus per head.

In the medium run, the increase in the current account surplus per head contributes to the accumulation of foreign bonds per head held by the private sector. That is why output per head continues to move up, and so does money demand per head. Owing to that, money per head held by the private sector climbs, foreign bonds per head held by the private sector drop, and foreign bonds per head held by the central bank climb. In due course the economy approaches a new long-run equilibrium. The current account surplus per head ceases to move. The same is true of foreign bonds per head held by the private sector, of foreign bonds per head held by the central bank, and of money per head held by the private sector.

Figures 1 until 3 plot the relevant time paths. First consider money per head held by the private sector, see figure 1. In the short run, it jumps up. Then, in the medium run, it keeps on rising. Second regard foreign bonds per head held by the private sector, see figure 2. In the short run, they are cut back. Then, in the medium run, they recover. And in the long run, they lie well above their initial level. Third take foreign bonds per head held by the central bank, see figure 3. In the short run, they spring up. Then, in the medium run, they continue to climb.

To better understand the working of the model, consider a numerical example. Let the parameter values be $c = 0.9$, $q = 0.3$, $n = 0.02$, $r = 0.04$, $i = 10$, $x = 30$ and $\kappa = 0.3$. The numercial example draws heavily on section 1.2. To simplify matters, let the money multiplier be unity. Originally the economy is in the steady state. Thanks to $m_1 = \kappa(y + rf)$, money per head held by the private sector is $m_1 = 30$. The foreign position is balanced $f = 0$. In $f = f_1 + f_2$, let be $f_1 = f_2 = 0$.

Against this background, exports per head go up from 30 to 31. First we shed some light on the momentary equilibrium. Money per head held by the private sector mounts up to $m_1 = 30.75$. On account of $\Delta f_2 = \Delta m_1$, foreign bonds per head held by the central bank are $f_2 = 0.75$. Corresponding to $f_1 = f - f_2$, foreign bonds per head held by the private sector are $f_1 = -0.75$. This can be interpreted as follows. Domestic residents hold foreign bonds, foreigners hold domestic bonds, and the net foreign position is -0.75.

Then we throw some light on the new steady state. Money per head held by the private sector is $m_1 = 31.5$. By virtue of $\Delta f_2 = \Delta m_1$, foreign bonds per head held by the central bank are $f_2 = 1.5$. And according to $f_1 = f - f_2$, foreign bonds per head held by the private sector are $f_1 = 23.5$. Clearly this is the dominating effect. Table 18 offers an overview.

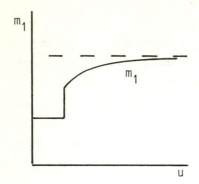

Figure 1
Money Supply Per Head

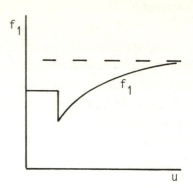

Figure 2
Foreign Bonds Per Head
Held by Private Sector

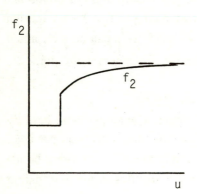

Figure 3
Foreign Bonds Per Head
Held by Central Bank

Table 18
Full Model
Increase in Exports Per Head

	1	2	3
x	30	31	31
f	0	0	25
y	100	102.5	104
y+rf	100	102.5	105
z	0	0.25	0.5
m_1	30	30.8	31.5
f_1	0	-0.8	23.5
f_2	0	0.8	1.5

1.8. Money Wages

In this section we shall give a brief sketch of the role played by money wages. In doing this, we shall proceed in four steps: fixed money wages, flexible money wages, slow money wages, and slow exchange rate policy cum slow money wages.

1) Fixed money wages. p denotes the price of domestic goods in terms of domestic currency. On the assumption of markup pricing, the price of domestic goods is proportionate to domestic money wages. p* symbolizes the price of foreign goods in terms of foreign currency. e is the nominal exchange rate, so ep*/p is the real exchange rate. x stands for exports per head expressed in domestic goods. Exports per head are an increasing function of the real exchange rate x =

jep*/p with sensitivity j = const. Set e = p* = 1, which involves x = j/p. Let domestic money wages be fixed. Then the price of domestic goods will be fixed, too. For ease of exposition, we assume that foreign assets are denominated in domestic goods (that is, foreign bonds are index bonds). f indicates foreign assets per head denominated in domestic goods.

The short-run equilibrium can be characterized by a system of two equations:

$$y = (c-q)(y+rf) + i + j/p \tag{1}$$
$$\dot{f} = j/p + rf - q(y+rf) - nf \tag{2}$$

Here $\dot{f}$ and y are endogenous. Solve equation (1) for output per head:

$$y = \frac{i + j/p + (c-q)rf}{1 - c + q} \tag{3}$$

Consider for instance a wage shock. An increase in money wages causes an increase in the price of domestic goods, thereby reducing both exports per head and output per head.

In the long-run equilibrium we have:

$$f = \frac{(1-c)j/p - qi}{(1-c+q)n - (1-c)r} \tag{4}$$

If the price of domestic goods is high, then foreign assets per head will be negative. Conversely, if the price of domestic goods is low, then foreign assets per head will be positive. In other words, the high-wage country will be a debtor, and the low-wage country will be a creditor. What is more, an increase in the price of domestic goods leads to a reduction in foreign assets per head.

Finally have a look at the dynamic effects of a wage shock. Regard an increase in the price of domestic goods. In the short run, this cuts back output per head. Then, in the medium run, foreign assets per head start to decline. Therefore output per head continues to fall. Figure 1 reveals the time path of output per head.

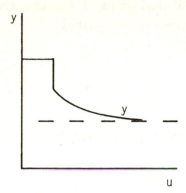

Figure 1
Wage Shock

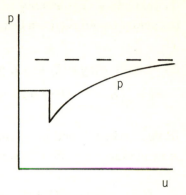

Figure 2
Flexible Money Wages

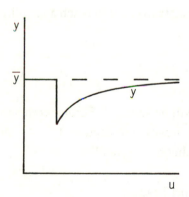

Figure 3
Slow Money Wages

2) Flexible money wages. Properly speaking, we assume that money wages (prices) adjust continuously so as to maintain full employment all the time. The temporary equilibrium can be represented by a system of two equations:

$$\bar{y} = (c-q)(\bar{y}+rf)+i+j/p \tag{5}$$

$$\dot{f} = j/p+rf-q(\bar{y}+rf)-nf \tag{6}$$

In this version $\dot{f}$ and p are endogenous. Equation (5) gives p, and (6) gives $\dot{f}$. Now rearrange equation (5) suitably:

$$j/p = \bar{y}-(c-q)(\bar{y}+rf)-i \tag{7}$$

A reduction in exports per head brings about a reduction in the price of domestic goods. The same applies to a reduction in investment per head. And an increase in foreign assets per head brings about an increase in the price of domestic goods.

The model can be condensed to a single differential equation. Eliminate j/p in (6) by means of (7) to verify:

$$\dot{f} = (1-c)(\bar{y}+rf)-i-nf \tag{8}$$

On this basis we can probe into stability. Differentiate (8) for f to reach a stability condition:

$$(1-c)r < n \tag{9}$$

Empirical evidence suggests that this condition will be satisfied. Further compare this to the condition obtained for fixed money wages, see section 1.1. As an outcome, flexible money wages increase (the likelihood of) stability.

The permanent equilibrium of foreign assets per head is:

$$f = \frac{(1-c)\bar{y}-i}{n-(1-c)r} \tag{10}$$

A reduction in exports per head has no influence on foreign assets per head. And a reduction in investment per head causes an increase in foreign assets per head.

Last but not least take a glance at the process of adjustment generated by two distinct shocks. First imagine a reduction in exports per head. In the short term, this lowers the price of domestic goods. Then, in the intermediate term, foreign assets per head remain unchanged. That is why the price of domestic goods does not move any more. Second think of a reduction in investment per head. In the short term, this depresses the price of domestic goods. Then, in the intermediate term, foreign assets per head begin to grow. This in turn enhances the price of domestic goods. And in the long term, the price of domestic goods rises well above its initial level. Figure 2 graphs the trajectory of the price of domestic goods.

3) Slow money wages. Let the rate of change of money wages be a decreasing function of the rate of unemployment $\dot{p}/p = -\lambda(\bar{y}-y)$. Here p denotes the price of domestic goods, $\bar{y}$ is full-employment output per head, y is actual output per head, $\bar{y}-y$ is the output gap per head, and $\lambda > 0$ is the speed of adjustment. The momentary equilibrium can be written as a system of three equations:

$$y = (c-q)(y+rf)+i+j/p \tag{11}$$

$$\dot{f} = j/p+rf-q(y+rf)-nf \tag{12}$$

$$\dot{p} = -\lambda p(\bar{y}-y) \tag{13}$$

In this case $\dot{f}$, $\dot{p}$ and y are endogenous. Equation (11) gives y, (12) gives $\dot{f}$, and (13) gives $\dot{p}$.

The steady state can be described by a system of two equations:

$$\bar{y} = (c-q)(\bar{y}+rf)+i+j/p \tag{14}$$

$$nf = j/p+rf-q(\bar{y}+rf) \tag{15}$$

Here f and p are endogenous. As a matter of fact, this is equivalent to the steady state obtained for flexible money wages.

Now catch a glimpse of transitional dynamics. First consider a reduction in exports per head. In the short run, as a response, output per head comes down. Then, in the medium run, the price of domestic goods starts to decline. For that reason, output per head goes up again. Second regard a reduction in investment per head. In the short period, this contracts output per head. Then, in the intermediate period, the price of domestic goods begins to fall. This in turn expands output per head. On those grounds, foreign assets per head begin to grow. Figure 3 shows how output per head evolves over time.

4) Slow exchange rate policy cum slow money wages. We posit that the rate of devaluation is an increasing function of the rate of unemployment $\dot{e}/e = \mu(\bar{y}-y)$. Here $\mu > 0$ indicates the speed of adjustment. The short-run equilibrium can be captured by a system of four equations:

$$y = (c-q)(y+rf)+i+je/p \tag{16}$$
$$\dot{f} = je/p+rf-q(y+rf)-nf \tag{17}$$
$$\dot{p} = -\lambda p(\bar{y}-y) \tag{18}$$
$$\dot{e} = \mu e(\bar{y}-y) \tag{19}$$

In this situation $\dot{e}$, $\dot{f}$, $\dot{p}$ and y are endogenous. Equation (16) gives y, (17) gives $\dot{f}$, (18) gives $\dot{p}$, and (19) gives $\dot{e}$.

The long-run equilibrium simplifies to a system of two equations:

$$\bar{y} = (c-q)(\bar{y}+rf)+i+je/p \tag{20}$$
$$nf = je/p+rf-q(\bar{y}+rf) \tag{21}$$

Here e, f and p are endogenous, so there is one degree of freedom. Equations (20) and (21) yield e/p and f. Then λ and μ determine e and p.

Take for instance a reduction in exports per head. In the short run, this diminishes output per head. Then, in the medium run, the exchange rate starts climbing, whereas the price of domestic goods begins to drop. This in turn augments output per head.

Coming to an end, we shed some more light on the dynamic aspects. We have $\hat{p} = -\lambda(\bar{y} - y)$, where $\hat{p}$ stands for the rate of change of p. Similarly we have $\hat{e} = \mu(\bar{y} - y)$. This provides:

$$\frac{\hat{p}}{\hat{e}} = -\frac{\lambda}{\mu} \tag{22}$$

If $\lambda > \mu$, then $|\hat{p}| > |\hat{e}|$. The other way round, if $\lambda < \mu$, then $|\hat{p}| < |\hat{e}|$. If λ/μ increases, then the change in prices, taken over the process as a whole, increases too. On the other hand, the change in the exchange rate declines. As λ/μ tends to infinity, the change in the exchange rate tends to zero. Conversely, as λ/μ tends to zero, it is the change in prices that tends to zero.

2. Economy with Public Sector (Public Debt)

2.1. Exogenous Fiscal Policy

In this section, the public sector will be incorporated into the model. The analysis will be carried out within the following framework. Let us begin with the assumptions concerning the public sector. The government fixes its purchases of goods and services on a per capita basis g = const. Then multiplying government purchases per head by labour supply gives the total of government purchases $G = gN$. Likewise the government fixes its deficit on a per capita basis b = const. Then multiplying the budget deficit per head by labour supply gives the budget deficit $B = bN$. The budget deficit in turn adds to public debt $\dot{D} = B$. Similarly the government fixes the tax on a per capita basis t = const. Then multiplying the tax per head by labour supply gives tax revenue $T = tN$. The government pays the interest rate r on public debt D, so public interest amounts to rD. The government budget identity has it that tax revenue equals government purchases plus public interest minus the budget deficit $T = G + rD - B$. Taking all pieces together, we arrive at $tN = gN + rD - bN$. Here the budget deficit per head and government purchases per head are exogenous, whereas the tax per head is endogenous.

We come now to the foreign sector. Exports are fixed on a per capita basis x = const. Then multiplying exports per head by labour supply gives the total of exports $X = xN$. Domestic residents earn the interest rate r on foreign assets F, so the interest inflow amounts to rF. The disposable income of domestic residents is the sum of factor income, the interest inflow and public interest, net after tax respectively $Y_d = Y + rF + rD - T$. Observe $T = G + rD - B$ to get $Y_d = Y + rF + B - G$. Further note $B = bN$ as well as $G = gN$ to find $Y_d = Y + rF + bN - gN$. Imports are a certain fraction of the disposable income of domestic residents $Q = qY_d$ with q = const. The current account surplus can be defined as the excess of exports and the interest inflow over imports $Z = X + rF - Q$. The current account surplus in turn adds to foreign assets $\dot{F} = Z$. From this one can conclude $\dot{F} = xN + rF - q(Y + rF + bN - gN)$.

Finally we address the goods market. Households consume a fixed share of disposable income $C = cY_d$ with c = const. Firms fix investment on a per capita basis $I = iN$ with $i = $ const. Domestic output agrees with the demand for domestic goods $Y = C + I + G + X - Q$. This can be restated as $Y = (c-q)(Y+rF+bN-gN)+iN+gN+xN$.

Relying on this foundation, the short-run equilibrium can be represented by a system of four equations:

$$Y = (c-q)(Y+rF+bN-gN)+iN+gN+xN \tag{1}$$

$$\dot{D} = bN \tag{2}$$

$$\dot{F} = xN+rF-q(Y+rF+bN-gN) \tag{3}$$

$$\dot{N} = nN \tag{4}$$

The endogenous variables are $\dot{D}$, $\dot{F}$, $\dot{N}$ and Y.

It proves useful to conduct the investigation in per capita terms. Accordingly the short-run equilibrium can be compressed to a system of three equations:

$$y = (c-q)(y+rf+b-g)+i+g+x \tag{5}$$

$$\dot{d} = b-nd \tag{6}$$

$$\dot{f} = x+rf-q(y+rf+b-g)-nf \tag{7}$$

In this version $\dot{d}$, $\dot{f}$ and y are endogenous.

Solve equation (5) for output per head:

$$y = \frac{i+g+x+(c-q)(rf+b-g)}{1-c+q} \tag{8}$$

It is evident that an increase in government purchases per head leads to an increase in output per head. The same applies to an increase in the budget deficit per head (or, for that matter, in foreign assets per head). Besides, equation (7) can be reformulated as follows. Eliminate $y + rf + b - g$ in equation (7) by means of equation (5) and reshuffle terms:

$$\dot{f} = \frac{(1-c)(x+rf)-q(i+b)}{1-c+q} - nf \qquad (9)$$

In the long-run equilibrium, both public debt per head and foreign assets per head stop moving $\dot{d} = \dot{f} = 0$. This together with (6) yields:

$$d = \frac{b}{n} \qquad (10)$$

In addition, substitute $\dot{f} = 0$ into (9) to obtain:

$$f = \frac{(1-c)x - q(i+b)}{(1-c+q)n - (1-c)r} \qquad (11)$$

Foreign assets per head are positive if and only if $(1 - c)x > q(i + b)$, taking $(1-c)r < (1 - c + q)n$ for granted. If the budget deficit per head is high, then foreign assets per head will be negative. Conversely, if the budget deficit per head is low, then foreign assets per head will be positive. Put another way, the high budget deficit country will be a debtor. It will run a current account deficit and a trade surplus. On the other hand, the low budget deficit country will be a creditor. It will run a current account surplus and a trade deficit. What is more, an increase in government purchases per head has no effect on foreign assets per head. However, an increase in the budget deficit per head causes a reduction in foreign assets per head. Of course, the same holds for a simultaneous increase in government purchases per head and the budget deficit per head.

Next we shall discuss the dynamic consequences for output per head of three policy measures:
1) A simultaneous increase in government purchases per head and the budget deficit per head.
2) An isolated increase in the budget deficit per head.
3) An isolated increase in government purchases per head.

1) Simultaneous increase in government purchases per head and the budget deficit per head, by the same amount, respectively. In the short run, as a response, output per head goes up. Then, in the medium run, foreign assets per head start to decline. That is why output per head comes down again.

Here the question arises whether, in the long run, output per head will fall below its initial level. To answer this question, differentiate (8) for b, taking account of (11). Let the condition $(1 - c)r < (1 - c + q)n$ still be fulfilled. Then the condition for $\partial y / \partial b < 0$ is:

$$(1-c)r +(c-q)qr > (1-c+q)n \tag{12}$$

By the way, this is identical to the condition established for $\partial y / \partial i < 0$, cf. section 1.1. In the numerical example, the condition will be satisfied $0.0112 > 0.008$. Henceforth let condition (12) be met. That means, in the long run, output per head will indeed fall below its initial level.

From the point of view of fiscal policy, this can be rephrased as follows. In the short run, fiscal policy reduces unemployment. But in the long run, fiscal policy increases unemployment! This seems to be an important result. Figure 1 shows the time path of output per head.

At last we shall touch upon two additional topics concerning the long-run equilibrium. First, the income of domestic residents per head $y + rf$ will fall even more. The reason for this is that both output per head and foreign assets per head will decline. Second, the simultaneous increase in government purchases per head and the budget deficit per head causes an increase in public debt per head and a reduction in foreign assets per head, as is well known. Yet will these two effects be of the same size $|\Delta f| = |\Delta d|$? According to (10) and (11), the multipliers are:

$$\Delta d = \frac{\Delta b}{n} \tag{13}$$

$$\Delta f = -\frac{q\Delta b}{(1-c+q)n-(1-c)r} \tag{14}$$

The comparison of (13) and (14) gives:

$$|\Delta f| > |\Delta d| \tag{15}$$

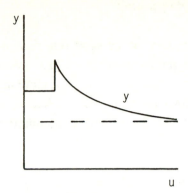

Figure 1
Increase in Government Purchases
and Budget Deficit Per Head

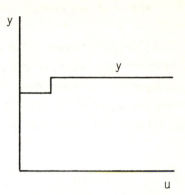

Figure 2
Increase in Government
Purchases Per Head

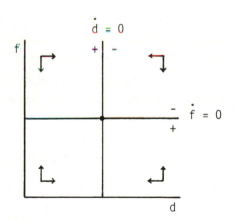

Figure 3
Phase Diagram

on the condition that $r > n$. As an outcome, the reduction in foreign assets per head will be greater than the increase in public debt per head.

2) Isolated increase in the budget deficit per head. In the short run, this government action raises output per head. Then, in the medium run, foreign assets per head begin to decumulate. This in turn lowers output per head. Once more the question comes up whether, in the long run, output per head will fall below its initial level. To solve this problem, differentiate (8) for b, paying attention to (11):

$$\frac{\partial y}{\partial b} = -\frac{(c-q)r}{1-c+q} \frac{q}{(1-c+q)n-(1-c)r} + \frac{c-q}{1-c+q} \tag{16}$$

The evaluation of (16) produces $\partial y / \partial b < 0$, given that $r > n$. In other words, in the long run, output per head will in fact fall below its initial level.

3) Isolated increase in government purchases per head (this is tantamount to the balanced budget multiplier). In the short run, the policy measure brings up output per head. Then, in the medium run, foreign assets per head are constant. Therefore, output per head will be constant, too. Figure 2 portrays the time path of output per head. The effect on output per head, however, will be rather small. A unit increase in government purchases per head causes a unit increase in output per head. Now compare fiscal policy to an export or investment shock. A unit increase in exports per head in the short run raises output per head by 2.5 and in the long run by 4, cf. section 1.2. A unit increase in investment per head in the short run raises output per head by 2.5. And in the long run, it lowers output per head by 2.

The next point refers to stability. The short-run equilibrium can be further condensed to a system of two differential equations:

$$\dot{d} = \varepsilon(d,f) \tag{17}$$
$$\dot{f} = \eta(d,f) \tag{18}$$

In the present case, equation (17) is particularly simple, cf. equation (6) $\dot{d} = b - nd$. Differentiate this for d to check:

$$\frac{\partial \dot{d}}{\partial d} = -n \tag{19}$$

Then set $\dot{d} = 0$ in $\dot{d} = b - nd$, which delivers:

$$d = \frac{b}{n} \tag{20}$$

Correspondingly figure 3 depicts the vertical $\dot{d} = 0$ demarcation line.

Equation (18) has already been determined, cf. equation (9). Differentiate this for f to verify:

$$\frac{\partial \dot{f}}{\partial f} = \frac{(1-c)r}{1-c+q} - n \tag{21}$$

Here a stability condition emerges:

$$(1-c)r < (1-c+q)n \tag{22}$$

This is identical to the condition obtained for an economy without public sector, cf. section 1.1. Let this condition be fulfilled, see above. Moreover set $\dot{f} = 0$ in equation (9) and regroup:

$$f = \frac{(1-c)x - q(i+b)}{(1-c+q)n - (1-c)r} \tag{23}$$

It is obvious that f does not depend on d. Correspondingly figure 3 reveals the horizontal $\dot{f} = 0$ demarcation line. The lesson taught by the phase diagram in figure 3 is that the long-run equilibrium will be stable.

Finally we shall trace out the process of adjustment induced by a simultaneous increase in government purchases per head and the budget deficit per head. At the beginning, the economy is in the long-run equilibrium. Let the budget be balanced, so there is no public debt $b = d = 0$. Likewise let the trade account and the current account be balanced, so there are no foreign assets $h = z = f = 0$. Output per head is invariant. In the phase diagram, the steady state is marked by the point of intersection, cf. figure 4.

Against this background, the government increases both its purchases per head and its deficit per head, by the same amount, respectively. In the phase diagram, the $\dot{d} = 0$ line shifts to the right, whereas the $\dot{f} = 0$ line shifts downwards. In the short run, the policy measure raises output per head. The budget gets into deficit. Imports per head go up, so the trade account and the current account get into deficit, too.

In the medium run, the budget deficit per head contributes to the accumulation of public debt per head. Similarly the current account deficit per head contributes to the accumulation of foreign debt per head. The swell in the interest outflow per head reduces the income of domestic residents per head, thereby lowering consumption per head and hence output per head. Besides, the fall in the income of domestic residents per head diminishes imports per head and thus the trade deficit per head. After a certain span of time, the trade account changes into surplus. In the phase diagram, the streamline indicates how the economy travels through time.

As time moves on, the economy approaches a new long-run equilibrium. The budget deficit per head and public debt per head come to a halt. The same applies to the current account deficit per head and foreign debt per head. Output per head is again invariant. Properly speaking, foreign debt per head exceeds public debt per head. Accordingly, the current account deficit per head surpasses the budget deficit per head. And output per head lies below its original level. In the short run, fiscal policy reduces unemployment. In the long run, however, it increases unemployment.

Figure 5 visualizes the autonomous path of the budget deficit per head as well as the induced path of the current account deficit per head. The process starts out with a one-time jump in the budget deficit per head. Owing to that, in the short run, a current account deficit comes into existence. Then, in the medium run, the current account deficit per head continues to rise. This is clearly reflected in the trajectories of public debt per head and foreign debt per head, see figure 6. Public debt per head grows period by period, and much the same holds for foreign debt per head.

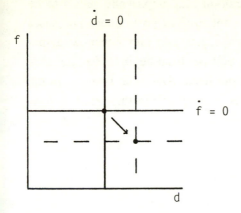

Figure 4
Increase in Government Purchases
and Budget Deficit Per Head

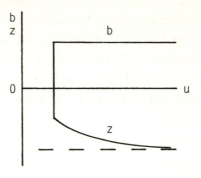

Figure 5
Budget Deficit and
Current Account Surplus Per Head

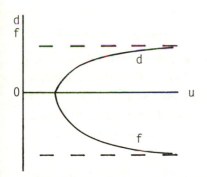

Figure 6
Public Debt and
Foreign Assets Per Head

In summary, there exists a stability condition that empirically seems to be sound. Consider for instance a simultaneous increase in government purchases per head and the budget deficit per head. In the short run, this enhances output per head. Then, in the medium run, foreign assets per head begin to decline. This in turn puts a downward pressure on output per head. And what is more, in the long run, output per head falls well below its initial level. In this sense, exogenous fiscal policy can be sustained.

2.2. Numerical Example

To better understand the working of the model, have a look at a numerical example. Let the parameter values be $c = 0.9$, $q = 0.3$, $n = 0.02$, $r = 0.04$, $i = 8$, $x = 24$, $g = 20$ and $b = 0$. Initially the economy is in the steady state. According to $d = b/n$, there is no public debt $d = 0$. And according to equation (11) from section 2.1., the foreign position is balanced $f = 0$. By virtue of equation (8), output per head is $y = 100$. And by virtue of the consumption function $cc = c(y + rf + b - g)$, consumption per head is $cc = 72$.

In these circumstances, the government raises its purchases per head from 20 to 21. At the same time, it raises the budget deficit per head from 0 to 1. In the short term, as a reaction, output per head improves from 100 to 102.5. Then, in the intermediate term, foreign debt per head accumulates slowly from 0 to 75. Due to that, output per head deteriorates round by round from 102.5 to 98. Put another way, the short-term multiplier is +2.5, and the long-term multiplier is −2.

Over and above that, in the intermediate term, public debt per head grows step by step from 0 to 50. The income of domestic residents per head in the short term rises from 100 to 102.5. But in the intermediate term it gradually falls back until it settles down at 95. Consumption per head in the short term goes up from 72 to 74. Then, in the intermediate term, it comes down to 68. The sum of consumption and government purchases, in per capita terms respectively, in the short term is pushed up from 92 to 95. Then, in the intermediate term, it is pulled down to 89.

The current account deficit per head in the short term climbs from 0 to 0.8. Then, in the intermediate term, it keeps on climbing until it reaches 1.5. The trade deficit per head in the short term mounts from 0 to 0.8. Then, in the intermediate term, it starts to descend. And in the long term it changes into a trade surplus per head of 1.5. The ratio of public debt to output d/y expands from 0 to 0.51. And the ratio of foreign debt to output f/y moves up from 0 to 0.77. Table 19 offers a synopsis.

Table 19
Fixed Exchange Rate
Increase in Government Purchases and Budget Deficit Per Head

	1	2	3
g	20	21	21
b	0	1	1
d	0	0	50
f	0	0	− 75
y	100	102.5	98
y+rf	100	102.5	95
cc	72	74.3	67.5
cc+g	92	95.3	88.5
z	0	− 0.8	− 1.5
h	0	− 0.8	1.5
d/y	0	0	0.51
f/y	0	0	− 0.77

2.3. Endogenous Fiscal Policy

In this section we suppose that the government continuously adjusts both its purchases per head and its deficit per head so as to maintain full employment all the time. Is this feasible? Define $w = g - b$ and let be $w = $ const. In full analogy to section 2.1. the short-run equilibrium can be characterized by a system of three equations:

$$\bar{y} = (c-q)(\bar{y}+rf-w)+i+g+x \tag{1}$$
$$\dot{d} = g-w-nd \tag{2}$$
$$\dot{f} = x+rf-q(\bar{y}+rf-w)-nf \tag{3}$$

Here $\dot{d}$, $\dot{f}$ and g are endogenous.

For purposes of stability analysis, the model can be viewed as a system of two differential equations:

$$\dot{d} = \varepsilon(d,f) \tag{4}$$
$$\dot{f} = \eta(d,f) \tag{5}$$

Get rid of g in equation (2) by making use of equation (1) to accomplish equation (4):

$$\dot{d} = \bar{y}-(c-q)(\bar{y}+rf-w)-i-x-w-nd \tag{6}$$

Then differentiate this for d:

$$\frac{\partial \dot{d}}{\partial d} = -n < 0 \tag{7}$$

Further set $\dot{d} = 0$ in equation (6) and rearrange:

$$nd = (1-c+q)(\bar{y}-w)-(c-q)rf-i-x \tag{8}$$

An increase in f calls for a decline in d, as can be learnt from equation (8). Correspondingly figure 1 graphs the downward sloping $\dot{d} = 0$ line.

In this instance, equation (5) is identical to equation (3). Now differentiate equation (3) for f:

$$\frac{\partial \dot{f}}{\partial f} = (1-q)r - n \tag{9}$$

In the numerical example we have $(1 - q)r > n$. Henceforth let be $(1 - q)r > n$, which implies $\partial \dot{f} / \partial f > 0$. Moreover set $\dot{f} = 0$ in equation (3) and regroup:

$$f = \frac{q(\bar{y} - w) - x}{(1-q)r - n} \tag{10}$$

Here f is independent of d. Correspondingly figure 1 plots the horizontal $\dot{f} = 0$ line. Judging by the directional arrows in the phase diagram (figure 1), the long-run equilibrium will be unstable!

To see this more clearly, we shall keep track of the process of adjustment generated by a permanent export shock. At the beginning, the economy is in the steady state. Let the budget be balanced, so there is no public debt b = d = 0. Likewise let the current account and the foreign position be balanced z = f = 0. Output per head is uniform. In this situation, exports per head drop. In the short run, leaning against the wind, the government increases both its purchases per head and its deficit per head. To the effect that output per head stays constant and full employment still prevails. In the phase diagram, the $\dot{d} = 0$ line shifts to the right, whereas the $\dot{f} = 0$ line shifts upwards, cf. figure 2.

In the medium run, the current account deficit per head contributes to the accumulation of foreign debt per head. Similarly, the budget deficit per head contributes to the accumulation of public debt per head. The expansion of the interest outflow per head contracts the income of domestic residents per head and thus consumption per head. To counteract this, the government continues to increase its purchases per head and its deficit per head. In the phase diagram, the

144

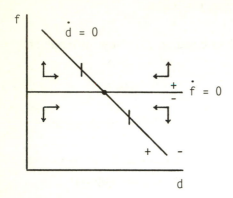

Figure 1

Phase Diagram

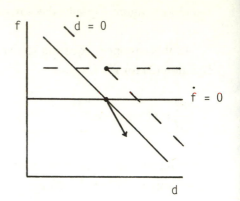

Figure 2

Endogenous Fiscal Policy

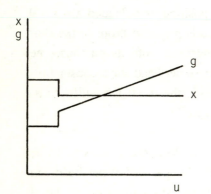

Figure 3

Exports and Government

Purchases Per Head

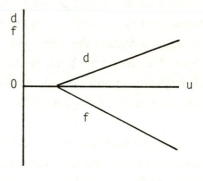

Figure 4

Public Debt and

Foreign Assets Per Head

streamline points out how the economy moves over time. In the long run, both foreign debt per head and public debt per head tend to explode.

Figure 3 contains the exogenous path of exports per head and the endogenous path of government purchases per head. There is a one-time cut in exports per head. In the short run, as a response, the government lifts its purchases per head. Then, in the medium run, the government continues to do so. Figure 4 in a stylized way exhibits the trajectories of foreign debt per head and public debt per head.

In summary, under endogenous fiscal policy, the long-run equilibrium will be unstable. Endogenous fiscal policy is effective in the short run, but it cannot be sustained. This is in remarkable contrast to the conclusions drawn for exogenous fiscal policy.

2.4. Slow Fiscal Policy, Slow Money Wages

The rate of change of government purchases per head is an increasing function of the rate of unemployment $\dot{g}/g = \mu(\bar{y}-y)$, where μ denotes the speed of adjustment. Apart from this we take the same avenue as before, cf. section 1.8. The temporary equilibrium can be described by a system of five equations:

$$y = (c-q)(y+rf-w)+i+g+j/p \tag{1}$$

$$\dot{d} = g-w-nd \tag{2}$$

$$\dot{f} = j/p+rf-q(y+rf-w)-nf \tag{3}$$

$$\dot{p} = -\lambda p(\bar{y}-y) \tag{4}$$

$$\dot{g} = \mu g(\bar{y}-y) \tag{5}$$

In this version $\dot{d}$, $\dot{f}$, $\dot{g}$, $\dot{p}$ and y are endogenous. Equation (1) gives y, (2) gives $\dot{d}$, (3) gives $\dot{f}$, (4) gives $\dot{p}$, and (5) gives $\dot{g}$.

The permanent equilibrium can be caught by a system of three equations:

$$\bar{y} = (c - q)(\bar{y} + rf - w) + i + g + j/p \tag{6}$$

$$nd = g - w \tag{7}$$

$$nf = j/p + rf - q(\bar{y} + rf - w) - nf \tag{8}$$

Here d, f, g and p are endogenous. There are four variables but only three equations, so we are left with one degree of freedom.

Next take a glance at transitional dynamics. Imagine for instance a reduction in exports per head. In the short term, this lowers output per head. In the intermediate term, to compensate for this, government purchases per head start to rise, whereas prices begin to fall. On this account output per head recovers period by period. Foreign assets per head decline, while public debt per head grows.

Last but not least, catch a glimpse of the part played by velocities. Equations (4) and (5) can be restated as $\hat{p} = -\lambda(\bar{y} - y)$ and $\hat{g} = \mu(\bar{y} - y)$, where the hat symbolizes the growth rate. From this one can deduce:

$$\frac{\hat{p}}{\hat{g}} = -\frac{\lambda}{\mu} \tag{9}$$

If $\lambda > \mu$, then $|\hat{p}| > |\hat{g}|$. Conversely, if $\lambda < \mu$ then $|\hat{p}| < |\hat{g}|$. Beyond that, if λ/μ goes up, then the change in prices, taken over the process as a whole, goes up as well. On the other hand, the change in government purchases per head (and in public debt per head) comes down. As λ/μ tends to infinity, the change in government purchases per head (and in public debt per head) tends to zero. The other way round, as λ/μ tends to zero, it is the change in prices that tends to zero.

3. Summary

To begin with, we assume an economy without public sector. First consider the basic model. The analysis yields a stability condition that empirically seems to be fulfilled. An increase in exports per head in the short run raises output per head. Then, in the medium run, foreign assets per head start to accumulate. That is why output per head continues to rise. An increase in investment per head in the short run brings up output per head. Then, in the medium run, foreign assets per head start to decline. This in turn cuts back output per head. In the long run, output per head falls below its initial level. In this sense, a fixed exchange rate can be sustained.

Second regard endogenous exchange rate policy. There exists a stability condition that empirically appears to be sound. A reduction in exports per head in the short run calls for an increase in the exchange rate, that is to say a devaluation. Then, in the medium run, foreign assets per head do not respond. So there is no further need to adjust the exchange rate. A reduction in investment per head in the short run calls for an increase in the exchange rate (i.e. a devaluation). Then, in the medium run, foreign assets per head begin to grow. To counteract this, the government must reduce the exchange rate (i.e. a revaluation). In the long run, the exchange rate falls below its initial level. In this sense, endogenous exchange rate policy can be sustained.

Third imagine flexible money wages. There is a stability condition that empirically seems to be met. A reduction in exports per head in the short run lowers prices. Then, in the medium run, foreign assets per head stay constant. Therefore prices do not move any longer. A reduction in investment per head in the short run deflates prices. Then, in the medium run, foreign assets per head start to build up. This in turn reinflates prices. In the long run, prices rise above their initial level.

So far we assumed an economy without public sector. Now we shall introduce the public sector (and public debt). First have a look at exogenous fiscal policy. There is a stability condition that empirically appears to be safe. A simultaneous increase in government purchases per head and the budget deficit per head in the short run expands output per head. Then, in the medium run, foreign assets per head begin to decline. This on its part contracts output per head. In the long run, output per head falls below its initial level. In this sense, exogenous fiscal policy can be sustained.

Second take a glance at endogenous fiscal policy. There exists a stability condition that empirically seems not to be satisfied. A reduction in exports per head in the short run calls for an increase in both government purchases per head and the budget deficit per head. Then, in the medium run, foreign debt per head starts to pile up. To compensate for this, the government must keep on increasing its purchases per head and its deficit per head. In the long run, foreign debt per head grows without limits. In this sense, endogenous fiscal policy cannot be sustained.

From the policy point of view, these findings can be summed up as follows. First, endogenous fiscal policy is effective in the short run. Unfortunately, however, it cannot be sustained. Second, monetary policy is ineffective even in the short run. The underlying reason is that the quantity of money is endogenous. Third, endogenous exchange rate policy is effective in the short run. And what is more, it can be sustained. Table 20 presents an overview.

Table 20
Fixed Exchange Rate
Stability of Long-Run Equilibrium

basic model	stable
endogenous exchange rate policy	stable
flexible money wages	stable
exogenous fiscal policy	stable
endogenous fiscal policy	unstable

CHAPTER II. FLEXIBLE EXCHANGE RATE

1. Economy without Public Sector

1.1. Foreign Assets Denominated in Domestic Currency

1.1.1. Basic Model

The investigation will be carried out within a small open economy characterized by perfect capital mobility. Let us begin with the foreign sector. e denotes the nominal exchange rate. p is the price of domestic goods, expressed in domestic currency. Similarly p^* is the price of foreign goods, expressed in foreign currency. So ep^*/p is the real exchange rate. F symbolizes foreign assets denominated in domestic currency. Hence F/p are foreign assets expressed in domestic goods.

Exports per head, stated in domestic goods, are an increasing function of the real exchange rate $x + jep^*/p$, where $x = $ const stands for autonomous exports per head, and $j = $ const is the sensitivity of exports per head with respect to the real exchange rate. It is convenient to set $p = p^* = 1$. Then F can be viewed as foreign assets in terms of domestic goods. Likewise $x + je$ can be viewed as exports per head in terms of domestic goods. Multiplying exports per head by labour supply gives the total of exports $X = xN + jeN$.

Domestic residents earn the interest r on foreign assets F, so the interest inflow amounts to rF. The income of domestic residents is made up of domestic income and the interest inflow $Y + rF$. Imports in terms of domestic goods are a fixed share of the income of domestic residents $Q = q(Y + rF)$ with import rate q = const. The current account surplus is the excess of exports and the interest inflow over imports $Z = X + rF - Q$. The current account surplus in turn adds to foreign assets $\dot{F} = Z$. Putting together these building blocks we arrive at $\dot{F} = xN + jeN + rF - q(Y + rF)$.

Now we come to the goods market. Households consume a certain fraction of their income $C = c(Y + rF)$ with consumption rate c = const. Let the import rate fall short of the consumption rate q < c. Firms fix investment on a per capita basis I = iN with investment per head i = const. Domestic output equals the demand for domestic goods Y = C + I + X − Q. From this one can deduce Y = (c − q)(Y + rF) + iN + xN + jeN.

Finally we address the money market. Money demand is an increasing function of the income of domestic residents and a decreasing function of the interest rate L = κ(Y + rF) − δrN. Here κ > 0 is income sensitivity, and δ > 0 is the sensitivity of money demand per head with respect to the interest rate. In what follows δrN will be suppressed. This can be justified on the grounds that the domestic interest rate agrees with the foreign interest rate r = r* = const, and that no interest shock does occur. Further, to simplify matters, set κ = 1. Accordingly money demand is L = Y + rF. The central bank fixes money supply on a per capita basis m = const. Then multiplying money supply per head by labour supply gives the total of money supply M = mN. In addition, money supply and money demand coincide mN = Y + rF.

Resting on this groundwork, the short-run equilibrium can be represented by a system of four equations:

$$Y = (c - q)(Y + rF) + iN + xN + jeN \tag{1}$$

$$mN = Y + rF \tag{2}$$

$$\dot{F} = xN + jeN + rF - q(Y + rF) \tag{3}$$

$$\dot{N} = nN \tag{4}$$

Here e, $\dot{F}$, $\dot{N}$ and Y are endogenous.

It proves useful to perform the analysis in per capita terms. Correspondingly the short-run equilibrium in per capita terms can be described by a system of three equations:

$$y = (c - q)(y + rf) + i + x + je \tag{5}$$

$$m = y + rf \tag{6}$$

$$\dot{f} = x + je + rf - q(y + rf) - nf \tag{7}$$

In this version e, $\dot{f}$ and y adjust themselves.

What are the principal attributes of the short-run equilibrium? To answer this question, solve equation (6) for output per head:

$$y = m - rf \tag{8}$$

An increase in money supply per head leads to an increase in output per head (which in general is not proportionate). However, an increase in investment per head does not affect output per head. The same applies to an increase in exports per head. And an increase in foreign assets per head leads to a reduction in output per head.

Next we shed some light on the exchange rate. Eliminate y in equation (5) by means of equation (6) and rearrange:

$$je = (1 - c + q)m - i - x - rf \tag{9}$$

Let be $(1 - c + q)m > i + x + rf$, since otherwise the exchange rate would be negative. An increase in money supply per head leads to an increase in the nominal exchange rate (i.e. a depreciation of domestic currency). Conversely, an increase in investment per head leads to a reduction in the nominal exchange rate (i.e. an appreciation of domestic currency). And the same holds for an increase in exports per head (or, for that matter, in foreign assets per head).

The short-run equilibrium can be further compressed to a single differential equation. Get rid of $x + je$ in equation (7) with the help of equation (5) and reshuffle terms $\dot{f} = (1 - c)(y + rf) - i - nf$. Then substitute equation (6):

$$\dot{f} = (1 - c)m - i - nf \tag{10}$$

On this basis we can probe into stability. Differentiate equation (10) for f to check:

$$\frac{\partial \dot{f}}{\partial f} = -n \tag{11}$$

In a growing economy, as a finding, the long-run equilibrium will be stable. In a stationary economy, on the other hand, the long-run equilibrium will be unstable. From this time on we posit a growing economy.

At this stage we leave the short-run equilibrium and turn to the long-run equilibrium. In the steady state, the motion of foreign assets per head comes to a standstill $\dot{f} = 0$. Put this into equation (10) and solve for foreign assets per head:

$$f = \frac{(1-c)m - i}{n} \tag{12}$$

f will be positive if and only if $(1 - c)m > i$. If money supply per head is large, then foreign assets per head will be positive. The other way round, if investment per head is large, then foreign assets per head will be negative. And autonomous exports per head have no influence on foreign assets per head. If the consumption rate is large, then foreign assets per head will be negative. But if the saving rate is large, then foreign assets per head will be positive.

In other words, the high-liquidity country will be a creditor, while the low-liquidity country will be a debtor. The high-investment country will be a debtor, while the low-investment country will be a creditor. The high-consuming country will be a debtor, whereas the low-consuming country will be a creditor. What is quite the same, the high-saving country will be a creditor, whereas the low-saving country will be a debtor.

Over and above that, an increase in money supply per head leads to an increase in foreign assets per head (due to a depreciation). On the other hand, an increase in investment per head leads to a reduction in foreign assets per head (owing to an appreciation). And an increase in autonomous exports per head leaves no impact on foreign assets per head (due to an appreciation). Beyond that, let the country in question be a creditor. Then an increase in the growth rate causes a decline in foreign assets per head. Instead, let the country be a debtor. Then an increase in the growth rate causes a decline in foreign debt per head.

What will be the dynamic effects of diverse shocks on output per head? First consider an increase in money supply per head. In the short run, this brings up output per head. Then, in the medium run, foreign assets per head begin to accumulate. This in turn brings output per head down again. Here the question arises whether, in the long run, output per head falls below its initial level. To solve this problem, insert equation (12) into equation (6) and regroup:

$$y = \frac{[n-(1-c)r]m+ir}{n} \tag{13}$$

Let $(1 - c)r < n$. Then, in the long run, an increase in money supply per head brings up output per head. That means, in the long run, output per head does not fall below its initial level. Correspondingly figure 1 shows the time path of output per head. In the short run, there is an upward jump in output per head. Then, in the medium run, output per head declines slowly. And in the long run, it settles at an intermediate level.

Second regard an increase in investment per head. In the short run, this does not affect output per head. Then, in the medium run, foreign assets per head start to decumulate. That is why output per head begins to grow. Figure 2 depicts the trajectory of output per head. Third imagine an increase in autonomous exports per head. In the short run, output per head does not respond. Then, in the medium run, foreign assets per head do neither accumulate nor decumulate. Therefore output per head stays constant. Fourth take an increase in the growth rate. Let the country in question be a creditor. In the short run, output per head remains unchanged. Then, in the medium run, foreign assets per head come down. This in turn raises output per head. Conversely, let the country be a debtor. In the short run, again, output per head stays fixed. Then, in the medium run, foreign debt per head diminishes. This in turn lowers output per head.

How does the exchange rate travel through time? First have a look at an increase in money supply per head. In the short run, as a reaction, the exchange rate goes up (i.e. domestic currency depreciates). Then, in the medium run, foreign assets per head begin to grow. By virtue of that, the exchange rate comes down again (i.e. domestic currency appreciates). Here the question arises whether, in the long run, the exchange rate falls below its initial level. To answer this question, dispense with f in equation (9) by making use of equation (12). The analysis produces a condition:

$$(1-c)r < (1-c+q)n \tag{14}$$

154

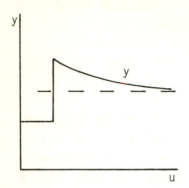

Figure 1
Increase in Money Supply Per Head

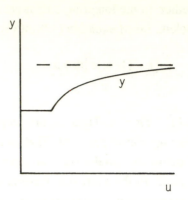

Figure 2
Increase in Investment Per Head

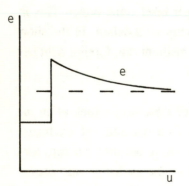

Figure 3
Increase in Money Supply Per Head

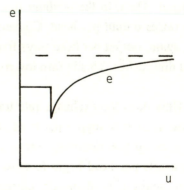

Figure 4
Increase in Investment Per Head

On this condition, in the long run, an increase in money supply per head enhances the exchange rate. By the way, (14) is reminiscent of the stability condition obtained under a fixed exchange rate. Let this condition be fulfilled. Then, in the long run, the exchange rate does not fall below its initial level. Figure 3 portrays the time path of the exchange rate. In the short run, the exchange rate is bid up. Then, in the medium run, the exchange rate is cut down gradually. And in the long run, it settles at an intermediate level. Clearly the time path is characterized by overshooting in the exchange rate.

Second take a glance at an increase in investment per head. In the short run, as a response, the exchange rate drops (i.e. domestic currency appreciates). Then, in the medium run, foreign assets per head start to decline. On that account, the exchange rate recovers step by step (i.e. domestic currency depreciates). Here the question comes up whether, in the long run, the exchange rate rises above its initial level. To solve this problem, combine equations (9) and (12). The analysis yields the condition $r > n$. On this condition, in the long run, an increase in investment per head lifts the exchange rate. Let this condition be met. Then, in the long run, the exchange rate in fact rises above its initial level. Figure 4 visualizes the trajectory of the exchange rate. In the short run, the exchange rate descends. Then, in the medium run, it mounts. And in the long run, it climbs above its initial level.

Third catch a glimpse of an increase in autonomous exports per head. In the short run, this depresses the exchange rate (appreciation of domestic currency). Then, in the medium run, foreign assets per head do not move. Thus there is no reason why the exchange rate should continue to move. That is to say, there is a one-time jump in the exchange rate.

The next point refers to the current account. Let z symbolize the current account surplus per head. Of course it holds $\dot{f} = z - nf$. Compare this to equation (10) to gain:

$$z = (1-c)m - i \tag{15}$$

If money supply per head is large, then the current account surplus per head will be positive. Put differently, the high-liquidity country will run a current account

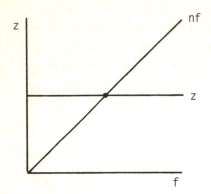

Figure 5
Current Account Surplus Per Head

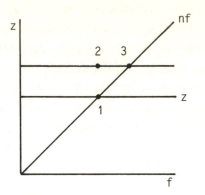

Figure 6
Increase in Money Supply Per Head

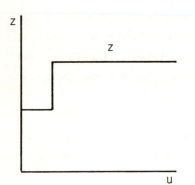

Figure 7
Increase in Money Supply Per Head

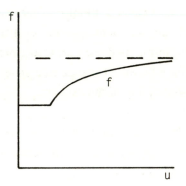

Figure 8
Increase in Money Supply Per Head

surplus. But if investment per head is large, then the current account surplus per head will be negative. Put another way, the high-investment country will run a current account deficit. What is more, an increase in money supply per head raises the current account surplus per head. The other way round, an increase in investment per head lowers the current account surplus per head. And an increase in autonomous exports per head has no consequences for the current account surplus per head.

According to equation (15), figure 5 reveals the current account surplus per head as a constant function of foreign assets per head. In addition figure 5 exhibits the nf ray. In the long-run equilibrium, foreign assets per head stop to adjust $\dot{f} = 0$. This together with equation (15) implies:

$$z = nf \tag{16}$$

In the diagram, the steady state is marked by the point of intersection.

Now we shall study the transitional dynamics of the current account and foreign assets. First consider an increase in money supply per head. At the beginning, the economy is in the long-run equilibrium. In figure 6, the steady state lies in point 1. Then the central bank augments money supply per head. In the diagram, the z line shifts upwards. The short-run equilibrium lies in point 2, and the long-run equilibrium in point 3. Properly speaking, z is the actual current account surplus per head. As opposed to that, nf is the current account surplus per head that is required to keep foreign assets per head constant. In the short run, the current account surplus per head exceeds the required level, so foreign assets per head grow period by period. Figures 7 and 8 display the time paths of the current account surplus per head and of foreign assets per head, respectively.

Second regard an increase in investment per head. In figure 9, the z line shifts downwards. In the short run, the current account surplus per head falls short of the required level, so foreign assets per head decline round by round. Figure 10 plots the trajectory of foreign assets per head.

Another point refers to the trade account. Let us begin with the short-run equilibrium. By definition we have $z = h + rf$, where h stands for the trade surplus per head. Amalgamate this with equation (15) to verify:

158

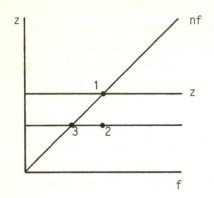

Figure 9
Increase in Investment Per Head

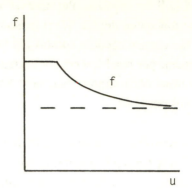

Figure 10
Increase in Investment Per Head

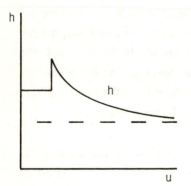

Figure 11
Increase in Money Supply Per Head

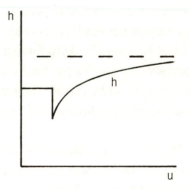

Figure 12
Increase in Investment Per Head

$$h = (1-c)m - i - rf \qquad (17)$$

It is evident that an increase in money supply per head in the short run leads to an increase in the trade surplus per head. An increase in investment per head leads to a reduction in the trade surplus per head. An increase in exports per head does not affect the trade surplus per head. And an increase in foreign assets per head leads to a reduction in the trade surplus per head.

We proceed now to the long-run equilibrium, where equation (12) applies. Eliminate f in equation (17) by means of equation (12) to reach:

$$h = -\frac{(r-n)[(1-c)m - i]}{n} \qquad (18)$$

If money supply per head is big, then in the long run the trade surplus per head will be negative. That is, the high-liquidity country will run a trade deficit. But if investment per head is big, then the trade surplus per head will be positive. That is, the high-investment country will run a trade surplus. What is more, an increase in money supply per head lowers the trade surplus per head. On the other hand, an increase in investment per head raises the trade surplus per head. And an increase in autonomous exports per head has no influence on the trade surplus per head.

Along these lines, figure 11 contains the time path of the trade surplus per head induced by an increase in money supply per head. In the short run, the trade surplus per head goes up. Then, in the medium run, it comes down again. And in the long run, it falls below its original level. Likewise figure 12 graphs the trajectory of the trade surplus per head generated by an increase in investment per head. In the short run, the trade surplus per head drops. Then, in the medium run, it recovers. And in the long run, it rises above its original level.

The salient features of the long-run equilibrium can be summed up as follows. The high-liquidity country will be a creditor. It will run a current account surplus and a trade deficit. By way of contrast, the high-investment country will be a debtor. It will run a current account deficit and a trade surplus.

Finally we shall trace out the process of adjustment in greater detail. First have a look at monetary policy. Initially the economy is in the long-run equilibrium. Let the trade account, the current account and the foreign position be balanced $h = z = f = 0$. Output per head is uniform. Against this background, the central bank augments money supply per head. In the short run, as a response, domestic currency depreciates. This in turn stimulates exports per head and output per head. The trade account gets into surplus, as does the current account.

In the medium run, the current account surplus per head contributes to the accumulation of foreign assets per head. On those grounds, domestic currency appreciates. This in turn puts a brake on exports per head and output per head. Moreover, the decline in exports per head lowers the trade surplus per head. After a certain span of time, the trade surplus changes into a trade deficit. Asymptotically the economy converges to a new long-run equilibrium. The current account surplus per head and foreign assets per head do not move any more. The same holds for the trade deficit per head. Output per head is again uniform. More precisely, the country has become a creditor. It runs a current account surplus and a trade deficit. For the time paths see figures 1, 3, 7, 8 and 11.

Second regard a (favourable) investment shock. At the outset, the economy is in the steady state. Let the trade account, the current account and the foreign position be balanced. Output per head is invariant. In these circumstances, investment per head jumps up. In the short term, domestic currency appreciates, thereby curbing exports per head. The net effect on output per head is that nothing happens. The trade account gets into deficit, as does the current account.

In the intermediate term, the current account deficit per head contributes to the accumulation of foreign debt per head. For that reason, domestic currency depreciates, thus advancing exports per head and output per head. Besides, the growth in exports per head reduces the trade deficit per head. After some time, the trade deficit turns into a trade surplus. As time passes away, the economy approaches a new steady state. The current account deficit per head and foreign debt per head cease to adjust. The same is true of the trade surplus per head. Output per head is again invariant. More exactly, the country has become a debtor. It runs a current account deficit and a trade surplus. For the time paths see figures 2, 4, 10 and 12.

In summary, the long-run equilibrium will be stable. First consider an increase in money supply per head. In the short run, this policy measure raises output per head. Then, in the medium run, foreign assets per head begin to accumulate. This in turn lowers output per head. But in the long run, output per head does not fall below its initial level. Second regard an increase in investment per head. In the short run, output per head does not respond. Then, in the medium run, foreign assets per head start to decline. That is why output per head starts to grow. Third imagine an increase in exports per head. In the short run, this shock has no effect on output per head. Then, in the medium run, foreign assets per head do neither accumulate nor decumulate. Therefore output per head stays constant. In this sense, a flexible exchange rate can be sustained.

1.1.2. Numerical Example

To illustrate the basic model, take a numerical example. Let the parameter values be $c = 0.9$, $q = 0.3$, $n = 0.02$, $r = 0.04$, $i = 10$, $m = 100$, $x = 20$ and $j = 10$. Initially the economy is in the long-run equilibrium. According to equation (12) from section 1.1.1., the foreign position is balanced $f = 0$. And according to $y = m - rf$, output per head is $y = 100$.

In this situation, the central bank augments money supply per head from 100 to 110. In the short run, this drives up output per head from 100 to 110. Then, in the medium run, foreign assets per head start to grow, rising slowly from 0 to 50. For that reason, output per head starts to decline, falling back slowly from 110 to 108.

The income of domestic residents per head in the short run jumps up from 100 to 110. Then, in the medium run, it remains at the higher level. The exchange rate in the short run is bid up from 1 to 1.4. Then, in the medium run, it is cut back to 1.2. Of course, the exchange rate varies more than in proportion to money supply per head. The current account surplus per head in the short run springs up from 0 to 1. Then, in the medium run, it does not move any more. The trade surplus per head in the short run expands from 0 to 1. Then, in the medium run, it contracts. And in the long run it turns into trade deficit per head of 1. Exports per head in the short run go up from 30 to 34. Then, in the medium run, they come down again. And in the long run they settle at 32. The ratio of foreign assets to output f/y in the medium run builds up from 0 to 0.46. Table 21 offers a synopsis. Column 1 gives the pre-shock steady state, column 2 the momentary equilibrium, and column 3 the post-shock steady state.

Table 21
Flexible Exchange Rate
Foreign Assets Denominated in Domestic Currency
Increase in Money Supply Per Head

	1	2	3
m	100	110	110
y+rf	100	110	110
f	0	0	50
y	100	110	108
e	1	1.4	1.2
z	0	1	1
h	0	1	− 1
x+je	30	34	32
ḟ	0	1	0
f/y	0	0	0.46
z/y	0	0.01	0.01

Second regard an increase in investment per head from 10 to 11, assuming money supply per head to be back at 100. In the short term, the shock leaves no impact on output per head. Then, in the intermediate term, foreign debt per head begins to accumulate, rising gradually from 0 to 50. On those grounds, output per head begins to grow, rising gradually from 100 to 102. Obviously the short-term multiplier is 0, and the long-term multiplier is 2.

The income of domestic residents per head stays constant at 100. The exchange rate in the short term is cut back from 1 to 0.9. Then, in the intermediate term, it is bid up to 1.1. The current account deficit per head in the short term jumps up from 0 to 1. Then, in the intermediate term, it does not change any more. The trade deficit per head in the short term expands from 0 to 1. Then, in the intermediate term, it contracts. And in the long term, it turns into a trade surplus per head of 1. Exports per head in the short term drop from 30 to 29. Then, in the intermediate term, they recover. And in the long term, they reach 31. The ratio of foreign debt to output $(-f/y)$ in the intermediate term swells from 0 to 0.51. Table 22 presents an overview of this process.

Table 22
Flexible Exchange Rate
Foreign Assets Denominated in Domestic Currency
Increase in Investment Per Head

	1	2	3
i	10	11	11
y	100	100	102
f	0	0	-50
y+rf	100	100	100
e	1	0.9	1.1
z	0	-1	-1
h	0	-1	1
x+je	30	29	31
$\dot{f}$	0	-1	0

So far we assumed that money demand depends on the income of domestic residents $L = \kappa(Y + rF)$. Now, for the sake of argument, we shall assume that money demand depends on domestic income $L = \kappa Y$. Without losing generality, let be $\kappa = 1$. Then in equilibrium we have $m = y$. In other words, domestic income per head will be governed by money supply per head. Imagine for instance an increase in investment per head. At first we posit $m = y$. Then domestic income per head will be constant. The income of domestic residents per head, however, will decline. So this is an adverse shock. Now, instead, we posit $m = y + rf$. Then domestic income per head will go up. But the income of domestic residents per head will be invariant. So this is a favourable shock.

1.1.3. Wealth in Consumption Function

In this section, wealth enters both the consumption function $cc = c(y + rf) + c\alpha f$ and the import function $qq = q(y + rf) + q\alpha f$. Let be $\alpha > 0$. The short-run equilibrium can be encapsulated by a system of three equations:

$$y = (c - q)(y + rf + \alpha f) + i + je \tag{1}$$

$$m = y + rf \tag{2}$$

$$\dot{f} = je + rf - q(y + rf + \alpha f) - nf \tag{3}$$

Here e, $\dot{f}$ and y are endogenous.

The model can be further condensed to a single differential equation. Eliminate je in equation (3) by means of equation (1) to get $\dot{f} = (1 - c)(y + rf) - \alpha cf - i - nf$. Then substitute $m = y + rf$ to achieve:

$$\dot{f} = (1 - c)m - \alpha cf - i - nf \tag{4}$$

What about stability? Differentiate equation (4) for f to realize:

$$\frac{\partial \dot{f}}{\partial f} = -\alpha c - n \tag{5}$$

Hence the long-run equilibrium will be stable.

In the steady state, the motion of foreign assets per head comes to a standstill $\dot{f} = 0$. This together with (4) provides:

$$f = \frac{(1-c)m-i}{n+\alpha c} \tag{6}$$

To illuminate this, consider a numerical example with $c = 0.9$, $q = 0.3$, $n = 0.02$, $r = 0.04$ and $\alpha = 0.01$. Table 23 points out the steady-state multipliers. The long-run effects on foreign assets per head prove to be smaller (in absolute terms). As regards output per head this is somewhat different.

Table 23
Wealth in Consumption Function
Long-Run Multipliers

α	0.01	0
$\partial f / \partial m$	3.4	5
$\partial y / \partial m$	0.9	0.8
$\partial f / \partial i$	− 34.5	− 50
$\partial y / \partial i$	1.4	2

1.1.4. Endogenous Monetary Policy

In the current section we postulate that the central bank continuously adjusts money supply per head so as to maintain full employment all the time. The short-run equilibrium can be enshrined in a system of three equations:

$$\bar{y} = (c-q)(\bar{y}+rf)+i+je \tag{1}$$

$$m = \bar{y}+rf \tag{2}$$

$$\dot{f} = je+rf-q(\bar{y}+rf)-nf \tag{3}$$

Here e, m and $\dot{f}$ are endogenous.

What are the key characteristics of the short-run equilibrium? To answer this question, have a look at equation (2). A reduction of investment per head does not call for a central bank action. And an increase in foreign assets per head calls for an increase in money supply per head. Next we throw some light on the exchange rate. Equation (1) can be restated as follows:

$$je = \bar{y}-(c-q)(\bar{y}+rf)-i \tag{4}$$

A reduction in investment per head leads to an increase in the exchange rate (i.e. a depreciation of domestic currency). And an increase in foreign assets per head leads to a decline in the exchange rate (i.e. an appreciation of domestic currency).

Now get rid of je in equation (3) with the help of equation (4) and regroup:

$$\dot{f} = (1-c)(\bar{y}+rf)-i-nf \tag{5}$$

On this basis we can check stability. Differentiate equation (5) for f:

$$\frac{\partial \dot{f}}{\partial f} = (1-c)r-n \tag{6}$$

This gives rise to the stability condition $(1 - c)r < n$. Let the condition be satisfied.

In the long-run equilibrium, foreign assets per head do not change any more $\dot{f} = 0$. Combine this with equation (5) to accomplish:

$$f = \frac{(1-c)\bar{y}-i}{n-(1-c)r} \tag{7}$$

If investment per head is high, then foreign assets per head will be negative. That means, the high-investing country will be a debtor.

At last we shall keep track of the process of adjustment kicked off by a reduction in investment per head. Initially the economy is in the long-run equilibrium. Let the current account and the foreign position be balanced. Each worker has got a job. In this situation, investment per head drops. In the short run, domestic currency depreciates, thereby stimulating exports per head. The net effect on output per head is that nothing happens. The labour market still clears. Apparently there is no need for the central bank to step in. And the current account gets into surplus.

In the medium run, the current account surplus per head contributes to the accumulation of foreign assets per head. That is why domestic currency appreciates. To prevent unemployment from coming into existence, the central bank augments money supply per head. Thus domestic currency depreciates again. With the lapse of time, the economy tends to a new long-run equilibrium. The current account surplus per head and foreign assets per head stop moving. Full employment does always prevail. Figure 1 shows the time path of foreign assets per head. And figure 2 shows the time path of money supply per head that is required to ward off unemployment.

How does the exchange rate travel through time? Take once more a reduction in investment per head. In the short run, this bids up the exchange rate. Then, in the medium run, foreign assets per head start to grow. This in turn cuts back the exchange rate. Here the question arises whether, in the long run, the exchange rate does fall below its initial level. To solve this problem, differentiate (4) for i, paying heed to (7). From the analysis emerges the condition $(1 - q)r > n$. Let this

168

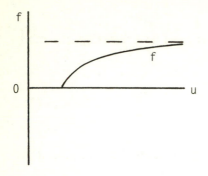

Figure 1
Reduction in Investment Per Head

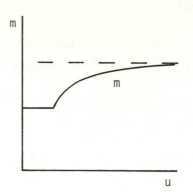

Figure 2
Endogenous Monetary Policy

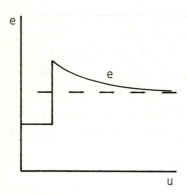

Figure 3
Exchange Rate

inequality be fulfilled. Then we arrive at $\partial e/\partial i > 0$. Put differently, in the long run, the exchange rate does not fall below its initial level. Figure 3 demonstrates how the exchange rate travels through time.

In summary, there exists a stability condition that empirically seems to be sound. Imagine for instance a decline in investment per head. In the short run, there is no reason why the central bank should change money supply per head. Then, in the medium run, foreign assets per head begin to accumulate. On those grounds, the central bank augments money supply per head. In this sense, endogenous monetary policy can be sustained.

1.1.5. Money Wages

In this section we shall give a rough outline of the role played by money wages. In doing this, we shall proceed in three steps: fixed money wages, flexible money wages, and slow money wages.

1) Fixed money wages. p denotes the price of domestic goods, expressed in domestic currency. We assume markup pricing, so the price of domestic goods is proportionate to domestic money wages. p* is the price of foreign goods, expressed in foreign currency. e is the nominal exchange rate, and ep*/p is the real exchange rate. x is exports per head, expressed in domestic goods. Exports per head are an increasing function of the real exchange rate $x = jep*/p$ with sensitivity j = const. It is convenient to set p* = 1, so we have x = je/p. Let domestic money wages be fixed, hence the price of domestic goods will be fixed, too. The central bank fixes the nominal quantity of money on a per capita basis m = const. The real quantity of money per head will be defined as m/p. For ease of exposition we suppose that foreign assets are denominated in domestic goods (that is, foreign bonds are index bonds). Thus f symbolizes foreign assets per head in terms of domestic goods.

Along the same lines as before, the short-run equilibrium can be characterized by a system of three equations:

$$y = (c-q)(y+rf) + i + je/p \tag{1}$$

$$m/p = y+rf \tag{2}$$

$$\dot{f} = je/p + rf - q(y+rf) - nf \tag{3}$$

Here e, $\dot{f}$ and y are endogenous.

What are the main properties of the short-run equilibrium? At first solve equation (2) for output per head:

$$y = m/p - rf \tag{4}$$

An increase in the price of domestic goods reduces output per head, as can be learnt from equation (4). We come now to the exchange rate. Dispense with y in equation (1) by making use of equation (2) and reshuffle terms:

$$je = (1-c+q)m - pi - prf \tag{5}$$

Initially, let the foreign position be balanced. Then an increase in the price of domestic goods lowers the exchange rate (i.e. domestic currency appreciates). Much the same applies to an increase in foreign assets per head.

In the long-run equilibrium it holds:

$$f = \frac{(1-c)m/p - i}{n} \tag{6}$$

If the price of domestic goods is high, then foreign assets per head will be negative. Conversely, if the price of domestic goods is low, then foreign assets per head will be positive. Put another way, the high-wage country will be a debtor, whereas the low-wage country will be a creditor. And what is more, an increase in the price of domestic goods reduces foreign assets per head.

Finally have a look at the dynamic effects of a wage shock. Strictly speaking, consider an increase in the price of domestic goods. In the short run, this depresses output per head. Then, in the medium run, foreign assets per head start to decline. This in turn enhances output per head. In the long run, output per head does not rise above its initial level. Figure 1 portrays the time path of output per head.

2) Flexible money wages. We start from the premise that money wages (and prices) continuously adjust so as to defend full employment all the time. The momentary equilibrium can be represented by a system of three equations:

$$\bar{y} = (c-q)(\bar{y}+rf)+i+je/p \tag{7}$$

$$m/p = \bar{y}+rf \tag{8}$$

$$\dot{f} = je/p+rf-q(\bar{y}+rf)-nf \tag{9}$$

In this version e, $\dot{f}$ and p are endogenous. Equation (8) gives p, (7) gives e, and (9) gives $\dot{f}$.

Now solve equation (8) for the price of domestic goods:

$$p = \frac{m}{\bar{y}+rf} \tag{10}$$

Let $\bar{y}+rf$ be positive. Then a fall in money supply per head lowers the price of domestic goods. A fall in investment per head has no influence on the price of domestic goods. The same is true of a fall in autonomous exports per head. And a rise in foreign assets per head lowers the price of domestic goods.

The model can be compressed to a single differential equation. Insert je/p from equation (7) into equation (9) and rearrange suitably:

$$\dot{f} = (1-c)(\bar{y}+rf)-i-nf \tag{11}$$

What about stability? Differentiate equation (11) for f:

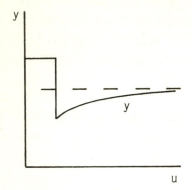

Figure 1
Wage Shock

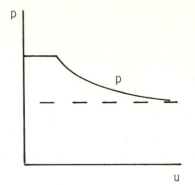

Figure 2
Investment Shock
(Flexible Money Wages)

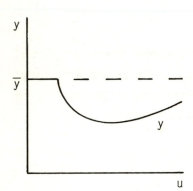

Figure 3
Investment Shock
(Slow Money Wages)

$$\frac{\partial \dot{f}}{\partial f} = (1-c)r - n \tag{12}$$

This leads to the stability condition $(1 - c)r < n$. Empirical evidence suggests that the condition will be fulfilled.

In the steady state we have:

$$f = \frac{(1-c)\bar{y} - i}{n - (1-c)r} \tag{13}$$

A fall in money supply per head does not affect foreign assets per head. A fall in investment per head raises foreign assets per head. And a fall in autonomous exports per head leaves no impact on foreign assets per head.

Coming to an end, take a glance at transitional dynamics. First consider a reduction in money supply per head. In the short term, as a response, the price of domestic goods drops. Then, in the intermediate term, foreign assets per head do not move. Therefore the price of domestic goods does not move either. Second regard a decline in investment per head. In the short term, the price of domestic goods remains unchanged. Then, in the intermediate term, foreign assets per head begin to grow. Owing to that, the price of domestic goods is cut back. Figure 2 exhibits how the price of domestic goods develops over time. Third imagine a decline in autonomous exports per head. In the short term, this has no effect on the price of domestic goods. Then, in the intermediate term, foreign assets per head do neither accumulate nor decumulate. Due to that, the price of domestic goods stays uniform.

3) Slow money wages. We postulate that the rate of change of money wages is a decreasing function of the rate of unemployment $\dot{p}/p = -\lambda(\bar{y}-y)$, where $\lambda > 0$ stands for the speed of adjustment. The temporary equilibrium can be described by a system of four equations:

$$y = (c-q)(y+rf) + i + je/p \tag{14}$$

$$m/p = y + rf \tag{15}$$

$$\dot{f} = je/p + rf - q(y+rf) - nf \tag{16}$$

$$\dot{p} = -\lambda p(\bar{y} - y) \tag{17}$$

Here e, $\dot{f}$, $\dot{p}$ and y are endogenous.

The permanent equilibrium can be condensed to a system of three equations:

$$\bar{y} = (c - q)(\bar{y} + rf) + i + je / p \tag{18}$$

$$m / p = \bar{y} + rf \tag{19}$$

$$nf = je / p + rf - q(\bar{y} + rf) \tag{20}$$

In this version e, f and p have adjusted themselves. By the way, this is identical to the conclusions drawn for flexible money wages.

At last catch a glimpse of the dynamic implications. First consider a fall in money supply per head. In the short run, output per head comes down. Then, in the medium run, the price of domestic goods starts to decline. By virtue of that, output per head recovers period by period. Second regard a fall in investment per head. In the short run, output per head does not respond. Then, in the medium run, foreign assets per head begin to grow. That is why output per head diminishes. This in turn lowers the price of domestic goods. Figure 3 visualizes the resulting trajectory of output per head. Third imagine a fall in autonomous exports per head. In the short run, this has no influence on output per head. Then, in the medium run, foreign assets per head do not stir. On that account, output per head and the price of domestic goods do not stir either.

1.2. Foreign Assets Denominated in Foreign Currency

1.2.1. Basic Model

In section 1.1., as a rule, we assumed that foreign assets are denominated in domestic currency. In section 1.2., in place of that, we shall assume that foreign assets are denominated in foreign currency. With this exception we shall take the same avenue as before. Here f symbolizes foreign assets per head denominated in foreign currency. So ef is foreign assets per head expressed in domestic currency. And ef/p is foreign assets per head expressed in domestic goods. To simplify notation, set $p = p* = 1$. Then ef can be viewed as foreign assets per head in terms of domestic goods. erf is the interest inflow per head in terms of domestic goods. $e\dot{f}$ is the change in foreign assets per head stated in domestic goods. And $q(y + erf)$ is imports per head stated in domestic goods.

The short-run equilibrium can be characterized by a system of three equations:

$$y = (c - q)(y + erf) + i + je \tag{1}$$

$$m = y + erf \tag{2}$$

$$e\dot{f} = je + erf - q(y + erf) - enf \tag{3}$$

Here e, $\dot{f}$ and y are endogenous.

What are the principal attributes of the short-run equilibrium? Let us begin with the exchange rate. Eliminate y in equation (1) by means of equation (2) and regroup:

$$e = \frac{(1 - c + q)m - i}{j + rf} \tag{4}$$

Set $(1 - c + q)m > i$. In addition, set $j + rf > 0$, even though f may be negative. These assumptions are sufficient for e to be positive. As a result, an increase in money supply per head raises the exchange rate (depreciation of domestic currency). On the other hand, an increase in investment per head lowers the exchange rate (appreciation). The same holds for an increase in exports per head (or, for that matter, in foreign assets per head).

We proceed now to output per head. Solve equation (2) for output per head and get rid of e with the help of equation (4):

$$y = \frac{jm + (c-q)mrf + irf}{j+rf} \tag{5}$$

Let $j + rf$ still be positive. First consider an increase in money supply per head. $j + rf > 0$ implies $j + (c - q)rf > 0$. Accordingly the increase in money supply per head raises output per head.

Second consider an increase in investment per head. If foreign assets per head are positive, then output per head will go up. Conversely, if foreign assets per head are negative, then output per head will come down. How can this be explained? Obviously two distinct effects are at work. The first effect has it that the increase in investment per head appreciates domestic currency, thereby curbing exports per head. On balance, output per head does not move. The second effect will be established for the case $f > 0$. The fall in the exchange rate reduces the interest inflow per head erf and hence the income of domestic residents per head $y + erf$. For that reason, money demand per head diminishes, too. This in turn enhances the exchange rate, exports per head, and thus output per head.

Third consider an increase in exports per head. This cuts back the exchange rate. Here, according to $y = m - erf$, two cases can occur. If $f > 0$, then erf will drop, so y will improve. However, if $f < 0$, then erf will climb, so y will deteriorate. Put differently, if the country is a creditor, then the increase in exports per head will raise output per head. The other way round, if the country is a debtor, then the increase in exports per head will lower output per head. This is in remarkable contrast to the findings for foreign assets denominated in domestic currency.

Besides, regard the special case that the foreign position is balanced. Then an increase in money supply per head brings up output per head. But an increase in investment per head leaves no impact on output per head. And the same applies to an increase in exports per head.

The model can be reduced to a single differential equation $\dot{f} = \varepsilon(f)$. Substitute je from equation (1) into equation (3) to verify $e\dot{f} = (1-c)(y+erf) - i - enf$. Then dispense with $y + erf$ by making use of equation (2):

$$\dot{f} = \frac{(1-c)m - i}{e} - nf \tag{6}$$

Further insert equation (4) and reshuffle terms:

$$\dot{f} = \frac{[(1-c)m - i](j + rf)}{(1-c+q)m - i} - nf \tag{7}$$

Having done this, we can inquire into stability. Differentiate equation (7) for f to arrive at a stability condition:

$$\frac{(1-c)m - i}{(1-c+q)m - i} < \frac{n}{r} \tag{8}$$

Equation (4) can be restated as:

$$(1-c+q)m - i = e(j + rf) \tag{9}$$

In the long-run equilibrium we have $\dot{f} = 0$. Put this into equation (6) to get:

$$(1-c)m - i = enf \tag{10}$$

By drawing on equations (9) and (10), the stability condition can be rewritten as enf/e(j + rf) < n/r. Let j + rf still be positive. Then the stability condition boils down to:

$$n > 0 \tag{11}$$

This is identical to the condition obtained for foreign assets denominated in domestic currency.

In the long-run equilibrium, the motion of foreign assets per head comes to a halt $\dot{f} = 0$. Combine this with equation (6) to reach foreign assets per head expressed in domestic currency:

$$ef = \frac{(1-c)m - i}{n} \tag{12}$$

This confirms the results acquired for foreign assets denominated in domestic currency. The high-liquidity country will be a creditor, while the high-investment country will be a debtor. And what is more, an increase in money supply per head causes an increase in foreign assets per head (expressed in domestic currency). On the other hand, an increase in investment per head causes a reduction in foreign assets per head. And an increase in exports per head has no influence on foreign assets per head.

The next point refers to output per head. Join equations (2) and (12) together to determine the steady state:

$$y = \frac{[n - (1-c)r]m + ir}{n} \tag{13}$$

This is equivalent to the conclusions drawn for foreign assets per head denominated in domestic currency. Let be $(1 - c)r < n$. An increase in money supply per head (in the long run) boosts output per head. The same comes true for an increase in investment per head. And an increase in exports per head does not impinge on output per head.

Now what are the dynamic consequences for output per head? First have a look at an increase in money supply per head. Owing to equation (5), the short-run multiplier amounts to:

$$\frac{\partial y}{\partial m} = \frac{j + (c-q)rf}{j + rf} > 0 \tag{14}$$

And due to equation (13), the long-run multiplier amounts to:

$$\frac{\partial y}{\partial m} = \frac{n - (1-c)r}{n} > 0 \tag{15}$$

That is to say, an increase in money supply per head drives up output per head, both in the short run and in the long run. Will the long-run effect be smaller than the short-run effect? The answer to this question is that it depends.

Take for instance the case that, initially, the foreign position is balanced. Then the impact multiplier is $\partial y / \partial m = 1$, and the steady-state multiplier is $\partial y / \partial m < 1$. Figure 1 displays the resulting time path of output per head. In the short run, output per head springs up. Then, in the medium run, it slowly falls back. And in the long run, it gravitates towards an intermediate level. Figure 2 portrays the time path of foreign assets per head (expressed in domestic currency). Initially the foreign position is balanced. Then foreign assets per head start to build up.

Second take a glance at an increase in investment per head. The short-run multiplier amounts to:

$$\frac{\partial y}{\partial i} = \frac{rf}{j + rf} < 1 \tag{16}$$

And the long-run multiplier is:

$$\frac{\partial y}{\partial i} = \frac{r}{n} > 1 \tag{17}$$

The long-run effect is bigger than the short-run effect, as can easily be seen.

Suppose that, initially, the country is a creditor. Then figure 3 exhibits the trajectory of output per head. In the short run, output per head goes up. And in the medium run, it continues to do so. Instead suppose that, initially, the country is a debtor. Then figure 4 reveals the trajectory of output per head. In the short run, output per head drops. In the medium run, it recovers. And in the long run, it rises above its initial level. Figure 5 shows the trajectory of foreign assets per head (expressed in domestic currency). Initially, let the foreign position be balanced. Then foreign assets per head start to decline.

180

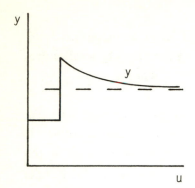

Figure 1
Increase in Money Supply Per Head
(Initial Value f = 0)

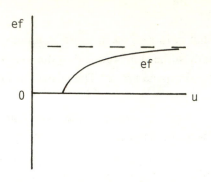

Figure 2
Increase in Money Supply Per Head
(Initial Value f = 0)

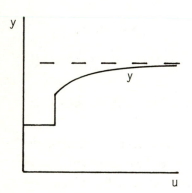

Figure 3
Increase in Investment Per Head
(Initial Value f > 0)

How does the exchange rate travel through time? To get ready, reformulate equation (4):

$$je = (1 - c + q)m - i - erf \tag{18}$$

Accordingly, in the short run, an increase in foreign assets per head (expressed in domestic currency) causes a reduction in the exchange rate.

First consider an increase in money supply per head. Initially, let the foreign position be balanced. Then, in the short run, the exchange rate is bid up. In the medium run, foreign assets per head (expressed in domestic currency) begin to pile up. Therefore the exchange rate is cut back. Here the question arises whether, in the long run, the exchange rate falls below its initial level. To solve this problem, differentiate equation (18) for m, observing equation (12):

$$\frac{\partial e}{\partial m} = \frac{(1 - c + q)n - (1 - c)r}{jn} \tag{19}$$

Let be $(1 - c)r < (1 - c + q)n$. Then we have $\partial e / \partial m > 0$. That means, in the long run, the exchange rate does not fall below its initial level. Figure 6 plots the time path of the exchange rate.

Second regard an increase in investment per head. Initially, let the foreign position be balanced. In the short run, the shock depresses the exchange rate. Then, in the medium run, foreign assets per head (expressed in domestic currency) start to decline. This in turn enchances the exchange rate. Here the question comes up whether, in the long run, the exchange rate rises above its initial level. Differentiate equation (18) for i, noting equation (12):

$$\frac{\partial e}{\partial i} = \frac{r - n}{jn} \tag{20}$$

Let be $r > n$. This involves $\partial e / \partial i > 0$. That is, the exchange rate indeed rises above its initial level.

Third imagine an increase in exports per head. Initially, again, let the foreign position be balanced. In the short run, the exchange rate descends. Then, in the

182

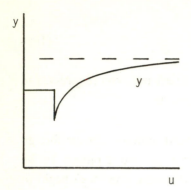

Figure 4
Increase in Investment Per Head
(Initial Value f < 0)

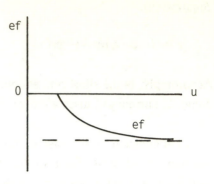

Figure 5
Increase in Investment Per Head
(Initial Value f = 0)

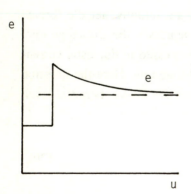

Figure 6
Increase in Money Supply Per Head
(Initial Value f = 0)

medium run, foreign assets per head (expressed in domestic currency) do neither accumulate nor decumulate. Thus the exchange rate does neither mount nor descend. In other words, there is a one-time jump in the exchange rate.

In summary, the long-run equilibrium will be stable. Take for instance an increase in money supply per head. Initially, let the foreign position be balanced. In the short run, the policy measure raises output per head. Then, in the medium run, foreign assets per head (expressed in domestic currency) begin to grow. This in turn lowers output per head. In the long run, output per head does not fall below its initial level. All of this underlines the importance of the conclusions drawn for foreign assets denominated in domestic currency.

1.2.2. Numerical Example

To elucidate this, consider a numerical example with $c = 0.9$, $q = 0.3$, $n = 0.02$, $r = 0.04$, $i = 10$, $m = 100$ and $j = 30$. Originally, the economy is in the steady state. Owing to equation (12) from section 1.2.1., the foreign position is balanced $ef = 0$. Due to (2), output per head is 100. And thanks to (4), the exchange rate is 1. In these circumstances, the central bank augments money supply per head from 100 to 110. In the short term, this lifts output per head from 100 to 110. Then, in the intermediate term, foreign assets per head expressed in domestic currency slowly build up from 0 to 50. That is why output per head shrinks back from 110 to 108.

The income of domestic residents per head $y + erf$ in the short term shoots up from 100 to 110. Then, in the intermediate term, it stays at the higher level. The exchange rate in the short term is bid up from 1 to 1.13. Then, in the intermediate term, it is cut back to 1.07. Exports per head in the short term go up from 30 to 34. Then, in the intermediate term, they come down to 32. Foreign assets per head expressed in foreign currency in the intermediate term accumulate from 0 to 47. Of course this is distinct from foreign assets per head expressed in domestic currency. Table 24 presents a synopsis of the process.

Table 24

Flexible Exchange Rate

Foreign Assets Denominated in Foreign Currency

Increase in Money Supply Per Head

	1	2	3
m	100	110	110
y+erf	100	110	110
ef	0	0	50
y	100	110	108
e	1	1.13	1.07
f	0	0	47
je	30	34	32

Instead, suppose that investment per head increases from 10 to 11. Let money supply per head be back at 100. In the short run, the shock has no effect on output per head. Then, in the medium run, foreign debt per head expressed in domestic currency grows step by step from 0 to 50. This in turn elevates output per head from 100 to 102. Apparently the short-run multiplier is 0, and the long-run multiplier is 2. The income of domestic residents per head remains unchanged at 100. The exchange rate in the short run drops from 1 to 0.97. Then, in the medium run, it climbs until it reaches 1.03. Exports per head in the short run contract from 30 to 29. Then, in the medium, they expand to 31. Foreign debt per head expressed in foreign currency piles up from 0 to 48. Table 25 offers an overview.

Table 25

Flexible Exchange Rate

Foreign Assets Denominated in Foreign Currency

Increase in Investment Per Head

	1	2	3
i	10	11	11
y+erf	100	100	100
ef	0	0	− 50
y	100	100	102
e	1	0.97	1.03
f	0	0	− 48.4
je	30	29	31

1.2.3. Full Model

Let us begin with the private sector. a_1 denotes assets per head held by the private sector, m_1 is money per head held by the private sector, b_1 is domestic bonds per head held by the private sector, and f_1 is foreign bonds per head denominated in foreign currency and held by the private sector. Hence the wealth identity of the private sector runs $a_1 = m_1 + b_1 + ef_1$.

We proceed now to the central bank. a_2 symbolizes assets per head held by the central bank, and b_2 is domestic bonds per head held by the central bank. The wealth identity of the central bank runs $a_2 = b_2$, and its balance sheet equation is $b_2 = m_1$. The central bank earns the interest rate r on its domestic bonds per head

b_2, so the interest earnings per head amount to rb_2. We assume that the interest earnings of the central bank are distributed to the private sector. Thus the income of domestic residents per head is $y - rb_2 + erf_1 + rb_2 = y + erf_1$.

The short-run equilibrium can be described by a system of eight equations:

$$y = (c - q)(y + erf_1) + i + je \tag{1}$$

$$m_1 = \kappa(y + erf_1) \tag{2}$$

$$b_2 = m_1 \tag{3}$$

$$b = b_1 + b_2 \tag{4}$$

$$a_1 = m_1 + b_1 + ef_1 \tag{5}$$

$$s = (1 - c)(y + erf_1) \tag{6}$$

$$\dot{a}_1 = s - na_1 \tag{7}$$

$$\dot{b} = i - nb \tag{8}$$

Here a_1, $\dot{a}_1$, $\dot{b}$, b_1, b_2, e, s and y are endogenous.

Equation (1) is the goods market equation, (2) is the money market equation, and (3) is the balance sheet constraint. Equation (4) gives the aggregate stock of domestic bonds per head. Equation (5) is the wealth identity. Equation (6) is the saving function, where s stands for savings per head. Equation (7) has it that savings add to the stock of assets. Likewise equation (8) has it that investment adds to the stock of domestic bonds. Equations (1) and (2) yield y and e, (3) gives b_2, (4) gives b_1, (5) gives a_1, (6) gives s, (7) gives $\dot{a}_1$, and (8) gives $\dot{b}$.

Now join equations (3) and (5) together $a_1 = b_1 + b_2 + ef_1$. Then pay heed to equation (4) $a_1 = b + ef_1$. Further put this as well as (6) into (7) $\dot{b} + e\dot{f}_1 = (1 - c)(y + erf_1) - nb - enf_1$. In equation (8) let be $i = nb$, which implies $\dot{b} = 0$. Taking all pieces together we come to $e\dot{f}_1 = (1 - c)(y + erf_1) - i - enf_1$. Accordingly the short-run equilibrium can be condensed to a system of three equations:

$$y = (c - q)(y + erf_1) + i + je \tag{9}$$

$$m_1 = \kappa(y + erf_1) \qquad (10)$$

$$\dot{ef}_1 = (1-c)(y + erf_1) - i - enf_1 \qquad (11)$$

In this version e, $\dot{f}_1$ and y are endogenous. As an important result, this is equivalent to the short-run equilibrium in the basic model, see section 1.2.1.

Suppose for instance that the central bank buys bonds. As a consequence, money per head held by the private sector rises. Domestic bonds per head held by the central bank rise, too, whereas domestic bonds per head held by the private sector fall. The subsequent depreciation increases exports per head, thereby enhancing output per head and the current account surplus per head. The depreciation means that the exchange rate goes up. This in turn raises foreign bonds per head expressed in domestic currency as held by the private sector (ef_1) and hence the total of assets per head held by the private sector.

2. Economy with Public Sector (Public Debt)

2.1. Foreign Assets Denominated in Domestic Currency

2.1.1. Exogenous Fiscal Policy

So far we considered an economy without public sector. Now the public sector (and public debt) will be incorporated into the model. First have a closer look at the public sector itself. The government fixes its purchases of goods and services on a per capita basis $g = const$. Then multiplying government purchases per head by labour supply gives the total of government purchases $G = gN$. Likewise the government fixes its deficit on a per capita basis $b = const$. Then multiplying the budget deficit per head by labour supply gives the budget deficit $B = bN$. The budget deficit in turn adds to public debt $\dot{D} = B$. Similarly the government levies a tax on a per capita basis $t = const$. Then multiplying the tax per head by labour supply gives tax revenue $T = tN$. In addition, the government pays the interest rate r on public debt D, so public interest amounts to rD. The government budget identity states that tax revenue must cover both government purchases and public interest, diminished by the budget deficit $T = G + rD - B$. Assembling all component parts, we achieve $tN = gN + rD - bN$. Here the budget deficit per head and government purchases per head are exogenous, while the tax per head is endogenous.

Second take a glance at the foreign sector. Exports are fixed on a per capita basis $X = jeN$ with sensitivity $j = const$. Domestic residents earn the interest rate r on foreign assets F, so the interest inflow amounts to rF. The disposable income of domestic residents is made up of domestic income, the interest inflow and public interest, net after tax respectively $Y_d = Y + rF + rD - T$. Substitute $T = G + rD - B$, observing $B = bN$ and $G = gN$, to get $Y_d = Y + rF + bN - gN$. Imports are a certain fraction of the disposable income of domestic residents $Q = qY_d$ with $q = const$. The current account surplus can be defined as exports plus interest inflow minus imports $Z = X + rF - Q$. The current account surplus in turn adds to foreign assets $\dot{F} = Z$. Putting all building blocks together, we gain $\dot{F} = jeN + rF - q(Y + rF + bN - gN)$.

Third catch a glimpse of the goods market. Households consume a given share of their disposable income $C = cY_d$ with c = const. Firms fix investment on a per capita basis I = iN with i = const. Domestic output coincides with the demand for domestic goods $Y = C + I + G + X - Q$. From this follows $Y = (c - q)(Y + rF + bN - gN) + iN + gN + jeN$.

Fourth we address the money market. Money demand is a specified proportion of the income of domestic residents $L = \kappa(Y + rF)$ with κ = const. Note that the income of domestic residents $Y + rF$ is distinct from the disposable income of domestic residents $Y_d = Y + rF + rD - T$. To simplify notation, let be $\kappa = 1$. The central bank fixes money supply on a per capita basis M = mN with m = const. Money demand aggrees with money supply $mN = Y + rF$.

Relying on this foundation, the short-run equilibrium can be characterized by a system of five equations:

$$Y = (c - q)(Y + rF + bN - gN) + iN + gN + jeN \tag{1}$$

$$mN = Y + rF \tag{2}$$

$$\dot{D} = bN \tag{3}$$

$$\dot{F} = jeN + rF - q(Y + rF + bN - gN) \tag{4}$$

$$\dot{N} = nN \tag{5}$$

Here e, $\dot{D}$, $\dot{F}$, $\dot{N}$ and Y are endogenous.

It is convenient to express the model in per capita terms:

$$y = (c - q)(y + rf + b - g) + i + g + je \tag{6}$$

$$m = y + rf \tag{7}$$

$$\dot{d} = b - nd \tag{8}$$

$$\dot{f} = je + rf - q(y + rf + b - g) - nf \tag{9}$$

In this version $\dot{d}$, e, $\dot{f}$ and y adjust themselves.

What are the main properties of the short-run equilibrium? To answer this question, solve equation (7) for output per head:

$$y = m - rf \tag{10}$$

An increase in government purchases per head has no effect on output per head. The same holds for an increase in the budget deficit per head. And an increase in foreign assets per head leads to a reduction in output per head.

Now we throw some light on the exchange rate. Eliminate y in equation (6) by means of equation (10) and rearrange:

$$je = (1-c+q)(m+b-g) - i - b - rf \tag{11}$$

Let be $(1 - c + q)(m + b - g) > i + b + rf$. An increase in money supply per head leads to an increase in the exchange rate (depreciation of domestic currency). On the other hand, an increase in government purchases per head leads to a decline in the exchange rate (appreciation of domestic currency). The same applies to an increase in the budget deficit per head (or, for that matter, in foreign assets per head).

Besides, we transform equation (9). Get rid of je in equation (9) with the help of equation (6) and reshuffle terms $\dot{f} = (1-c)(y+rf+b-g) - i - b - nf$. Then insert equation (7):

$$\dot{f} = (1-c)(m+b-g) - i - b - nf \tag{12}$$

At this stage we close the short-run equilibrium and open up the long-run equilibrium. In the steady state, the motion of public debt per head and foreign assets per head comes to a halt $\dot{d} = \dot{f} = 0$. This together with equation (8) delivers:

$$d = \frac{b}{n} \tag{13}$$

An increase in money supply per head has no influence on public debt per head. And a simultaneous increase in government purchases per head and the budget deficit per head (by the same amount, respectively) leads to an increase in public debt per head.

Further combine $\dot{f} = 0$ with equation (12) and solve for foreign assets per head:

$$f = \frac{(1-c)(m+b-g)-i-b}{n} \tag{14}$$

Obviously, the high-liquidity country will be a creditor, whereas the low-liquidity country will be a debtor. The other way round, the high government purchases country will be a debtor, whereas the low government purchases country will be a creditor. In full analogy, the high budget deficit country will be a debtor, whereas the low budget deficit country will be a creditor. And what is more, an increase in money supply per head leads to an increase in foreign assets per head. However, an increase in government purchases per head leads to a reduction in foreign assets per head. The same is true of an increase in the budget deficit per head.

Next we come to the dynamics of output per head. Take for instance a simultaneous increase in government purchases per head and the budget deficit per head. In the short run, this leaves no impact on output per head. Then, in the medium run, foreign assets per head start to decline. Therefore output per head starts to grow. Figure 1 contains the time path of foreign assets per head, and figure 2 that of output per head.

How does the exchange rate move over time? Take once more a simultaneous increase in government purchases per head and the budget deficit per head. In the short run, the exchange rate is cut back. Then, in the medium run, foreign assets per head begin to decumulate. That is why the exchange rate is bid up again. Here the question comes up whether, in the long run, the exchange rate rises above its initial level. To solve this problem, differentiate equation (11) for g, taking account of equation (14):

$$\frac{\partial e}{\partial g} = \frac{r-n}{jn} \tag{15}$$

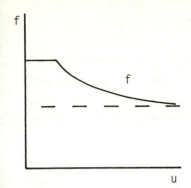

Figure 1
Increase in Government Purchases
and Budget Deficit Per Head

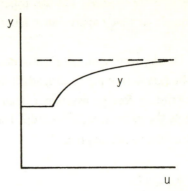

Figure 2
Output Per Head

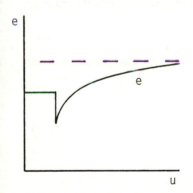

Figure 3
Exchange Rate

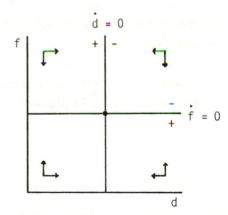

Figure 4
Phase Diagram

As a corollary, in the long run, the exchange rate in fact rises above its initial level. Figure 3 points out the trajectory of the exchange rate. In the short run, domestic currency appreciates. But in the long run, it depreciates.

By the way, a simultaneous increase in government purchases per head and the budget deficit per head leads to both an increase in public debt per head and a reduction in foreign assets per head, as has just been argued. Now are these two effects the same size $|\Delta f| = |\Delta d|$? Take differences of equations (13) and (14), respectively, to accomplish:

$$\Delta d = \frac{\Delta g}{n} \tag{16}$$

$$\Delta f = -\frac{\Delta g}{n} \tag{17}$$

From equations (16) and (17) one can deduce:

$$\Delta f = -\Delta d \tag{18}$$

As a result, the changes in public debt per head and foreign assets per head are the same size. This differs remarkably from the conclusions drawn under a fixed exchange rate. There the reduction in foreign assets per head exceeds the increase in public debt per head.

Moreover we shall discuss stability. The model can be interpreted as a system of two differential equations:

$$\dot{d} = \varepsilon(d, f) \tag{19}$$
$$\dot{f} = \eta(d, f) \tag{20}$$

In the present case, equation (19) is already well known $\dot{d} = b - nd$. Differentiate this for d to ascertain:

$$\frac{\partial \dot{d}}{\partial d} = -n < 0 \tag{21}$$

$\dot{d} = b - nd$ in conjunction with $\dot{d} = 0$ yields:

$$d = \frac{b}{n} \tag{22}$$

As an outcome, d does not depend on f. Correspondingly figure 4 portrays the vertical $\dot{d} = 0$ line.

Equation (20) is also quite familiar, cf. equation (12). Differentiate this equation for f to realize:

$$\frac{\partial \dot{f}}{\partial f} = -n < 0 \tag{23}$$

Then put $\dot{f} = 0$ into equation (12) and regroup:

$$f = \frac{(1-c)(m+b-g)-i-b}{n} \tag{24}$$

As a finding, f is independent of d. Correspondingly figure 4 portrays the horizontal $\dot{f} = 0$ line. The lesson taught by the directional arrows in figure 4 is that the long-run equilibrium will be stable.

Finally we shall trace out the process of adjustment induced by a simultaneous increase in government purchases per head and the budget deficit per head. At the beginning the economy is in the long-run equilibrium. Let the budget be balanced, so there exists no public debt. Likewise let the trade account and the current account be balanced, so the foreign position is balanced, too. Output per head is invariant. In the phase diagram, the steady state is marked by the point of intersection, cf. figure 5.

In this situation, the government enhances both its purchases per head and its deficit per head, by the same amount, respectively. In the phase diagram, the $\dot{d} = 0$ line shifts to the right, whereas the $\dot{f} = 0$ line shifts downwards. In the short run, the policy measure appreciates domestic currency, which on its part curbs exports per head. The net effect is that output per head does not respond. The budget gets into deficit, as do the trade account and the current account.

196

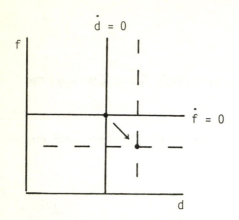

Figure 5
Increase in Government Purchases
and Budget Deficit Per Head

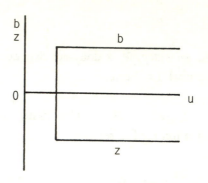

Figure 6
Budget Deficit and
Current Account Surplus Per Head

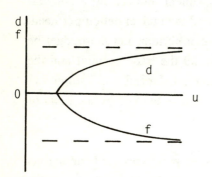

Figure 7
Public Debt and
Foreign Assets Per Head

In the medium run, the budget deficit per head contributes to the accumulation of public debt per head. Similarly the current account deficit per head contributes to the accumulation of foreign debt per head. The growth of foreign debt per head in turn causes a depreciation, thereby advancing exports per head and output per head. Moreover, the rise in exports per head leads to a fall in the trade deficit per head. Therefore, after a certain interval of time, the trade deficit is converted into a surplus. In the phase diagram, the streamline indicates how the economy develops over time.

In due course the economy approaches a new long-run equilibrium. The budget deficit per head and public debt per head stop moving. The same holds for the current account deficit per head and foreign debt per head. Strictly speaking, foreign debt per head equals public debt per head. Analogously, the current account deficit per head equals the budget deficit per head.

For the time paths, see figures 1, 2 and 3. In addition, figure 6 shows the autonomous path of the budget deficit per head as well as the induced path of the current account deficit per head. This is clearly reflected in the trajectories of public debt per head and foreign debt per head, cf. figure 7. Incidentally, it does not come by surprise that endogenous fiscal policy, as opposed to exogenous fiscal policy, is ineffective.

In summary, the long-run equilibrium will be stable. Regard for instance a simultaneous increase in government purchases per head and the budget deficit per head. In the short run, the government action leaves no impact on output per head. Then, in the medium run, foreign assets per head start to decline. This in turn brings up output per head. In this sense, exogenous fiscal policy can be sustained.

198

2.1.2. Numerical Example

To clarify exogenous fiscal policy, have a look at a numerical example. Let the parameter values be $c = 0.9$, $q = 0.3$, $n = 0.02$, $r = 0.04$, $m = 100$, $i = 8$, $g = 20$, $b = 0$ and $j = 24$. Initially the economy is in the steady state. Owing to $d = b/n$, there exists no public debt $d = 0$. By virtue of equation (14) from section 2.1.1., the foreign position is balanced $f = 0$. Thanks to $y = m - rf$, output per head is $y = 100$. According to the consumption function $cc = c(y + rf + b - g)$, consumption per head is $cc = 72$. And due to equation (11), the exchange rate amounts to $e = 1$.

Against this background, the government raises its purchases per head from 20 to 21. At the same time, the government raises its deficit per head from 0 to 1. In the short term, this has no influence on output per head. Then, in the intermediate term, foreign debt per head comes into existence, slowly building up from 0 to 50. For that reason, output per head slowly expands from 100 to 102. In other words, the short-term multiplier is 0, while the long-term multiplier is 2. Simultaneously public debt per head comes into existence, piling up round by round until it reaches 50.

Of course, the income of domestic residents per head stays constant at $y + rf = 100$. Consumption per head remains fixed at $cc = 72$. The sum of consumption per head and government purchases per head in the short term goes up from 92 to 93. Then, in the intermediate term, it is uniform at 93. The exchange rate in the short term is cut back from 1 to 0.96. Then, in the intermediate term, it is bid up to 1.04. The current account deficit per head in the short term jumps up from 0 to 1. Then, in the intermediate term, it settles at the higher level. The trade deficit per head in the short term is pushed up from 0 to 1. Then, in the intermediate term, it is pulled down again. And in the long term, it is converted into a trade surplus per head of 1. Exports per head in the short term drop from 24 to 23. Then, in the intermediate term, they climb up to 25. The reader may wish to refer to table 26.

As a rule, we assumed that money demand is based on the income of domestic residents $L = \kappa(Y + rF)$. As an exception, instead, we shall suppose that money demand is based on domestic income $L = \kappa Y$. Without loss of generality, let be $\kappa = 1$. The money market clears $m = y$. That is to say, domestic income per head will be controlled by money supply per head. Now imagine an increase in both government purchases per head and the budget deficit per head. This does not affect domestic income per head and lowers the income of domestic residents per head. Hence fiscal policy proves to be an adverse shock. In the standard model, however, the government action raises domestic income per head and does not impinge on the income of domestic residents per head. Hence fiscal policy proves to be a favourable shock.

Table 26
Flexible Exchange Rate
Foreign Assets Denominated in Domestic Currency
Increase in Government Purchases and Budget Deficit Per Head

	1	2	3
g	20	21	21
b	0	1	1
y	100	100	102
d	0	0	50
f	0	0	− 50
y+rf	100	100	100
cc	72	72	72
cc+g	92	93	93
e	1	0.96	1.04
z	0	− 1	− 1
h	0	− 1	1
je	24	23	25

2.2. Foreign Assets Denominated in Foreign Currency

(Exogenous Fiscal Policy)

Without losing generality we suppress investment per head $i = 0$. The short-run equilibrium can be encapsulated in a system of four equations:

$$y = (c - q)(y + erf + b - g) + g + je \tag{1}$$

$$m = y + erf \tag{2}$$

$$\dot{d} = b - nd \tag{3}$$

$$e\dot{f} = je + erf - q(y + erf + b - g) - enf \tag{4}$$

Here $\dot{d}$, e, $\dot{f}$ and y are endogenous.

What are the salient features of the momentary equilibrium? Let us begin with the exchange rate. Get rid of y in equation (1) with the help of equation (2):

$$e = \frac{(1 - c + q)(m + b - g) - b}{j + rf} \tag{5}$$

Assume $(1 - c + q)(m + b - g) > b$ as well as $j + rf > 0$, so e will be positive. An increase in money supply per head causes an increase in the exchange rate (depreciation of domestic currency). Conversely, an increase in government purchases per head causes a reduction in the exchange rate (appreciation of domestic currency). The same applies to an increase in the budget deficit per head (or, for that matter, in foreign assets per head f).

We address now output per head. Reshuffle terms in equation (2):

$$y = m - erf \tag{6}$$

A simultaneous increase in government purchases per head and the budget deficit per head cuts back the exchange rate. If the country is a creditor, then output per head will go up. If the foreign position is balanced, then output per head will not respond. And if the country is a debtor, then output per head will come down.

It is suitable to dispense with e in equation (4). Solve equation (1) for je and insert the resulting term into equation (4). Then take account of equation (2):

$$\dot{f} = \frac{(1-c)(m+b-g)-b}{e} - nf \tag{7}$$

Finally combine this with equation (5):

$$\dot{f} = \frac{[(1-c)(m+b-g)-b](j+rf)}{(1-c+q)(m+b-g)-b} - nf \tag{8}$$

This completes the proof.

In the steady state, the motion of public debt per head and foreign assets per head comes to a standstill $\dot{d} = \dot{f} = 0$. This together with equation (3) gives:

$$d = \frac{b}{n} \tag{9}$$

An increase in money supply per head has no effect on public debt per head. And a simultaneous increase in government purchases per head and the budget deficit per head causes an increase in public debt per head.

Further set $\dot{f} = 0$ in equation (7) to find out foreign assets per head denominated in foreign currency and expressed in domestic currency:

$$ef = \frac{(1-c)(m+b-g)-b}{n} \tag{10}$$

This is identical to the results obtained for denomination in domestic currency, cf. section 2.1.1. The high-liquidity country will be a creditor. On the other hand, the high government purchases country will be a debtor. And the same holds for the high budget deficit country. What is more, an increase in money supply per head causes an increase in foreign assets per head. However, an increase in government purchases per head causes a reduction in foreign assets per head. And the same is true of an increase in the budget deficit per head.

Next have a look at the dynamics of output per head. Initially, let the foreign position be balanced. Suppose that the government raises both its purchases per head and its deficit per head. In the short run, this leaves no impact on output per head. Then, in the medium run, foreign assets per head start to decline. Therefore output per head starts to grow. Correspondingly, figures 1 and 2 show the time paths.

How does the exchange rate float through time? Equation (5) can be reformulated as:

$$je = (1-c+q)(m+b-g)-b-erf \tag{11}$$

Hence an increase in foreign assets per head (expressed in domestic currency) causes a reduction in the exchange rate. Now consider a simultaneous increase in government purchases per head and the budget deficit per head. Initially, let the foreign position be balanced. Then, in the short run, the exchange rate is cut back. In the medium run, foreign assets per head (expressed in domestic currency) begin to accumulate. That is why the exchange rate is bid up again.

Here the question emerges whether, in the long run, the exchange rate rises above its initial level. To answer this question, take a glance at the steady-state multiplier. Differentiate equation (11) for g, paying heed to equation (10):

$$\frac{\partial e}{\partial g} = \frac{r-n}{jn} \tag{12}$$

Let be $r > n$, thus we have $\partial e / \partial g > 0$. That means, a simultaneous increase in g and b drives up e. Put another way, in the long run, the exchange rate indeed rises above its initial level. Figure 3 plots the trajectory of the exchange rate. It reminds one of the trajectory for denomination in domestic currency.

A simultaneous increase in government purchases per head and the budget deficit per head causes an increase in public debt per head as well as a reduction in foreign assets per head (expressed in domestic currency), as has just been ar-

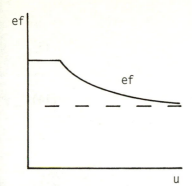

Figure 1
Increase in Government Purchases
and Budget Deficit Per Head

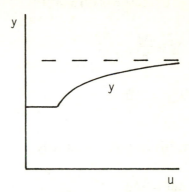

Figure 2
Output Per Head

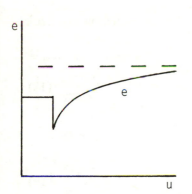

Figure 3
Exchange Rate

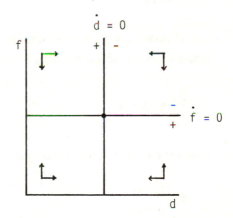

Figure 4
Phase Diagram

gued. But are these two effects the same size? To solve this problem, take diffe-rences of equations (9) and (10):

$$\Delta d = \frac{\Delta g}{n} \tag{13}$$

$$\Delta ef = -\frac{\Delta g}{n} \tag{14}$$

From this follows immediately:

$$\Delta ef = -\Delta d \tag{15}$$

In other words, the reduction in foreign assets per head (expressed in domestic currency) equals the increase in public debt per head.

Coming to an end, we shall examine long-run stability. The short-run equili-brium can be enshrined in a system of two differential equations:

$$\dot{d} = \varepsilon(d, f) \tag{16}$$
$$\dot{f} = \eta(d, f) \tag{17}$$

In this instance we are quite familiar with equation (16), see equation (3). Diffe-rentiate $\dot{d} = b - nd$ for d to get:

$$\frac{\partial \dot{d}}{\partial d} = -n < 0 \tag{18}$$

Moreover set $\dot{d} = 0$ into $\dot{d} = b - nd$:

$$d = \frac{b}{n} \tag{19}$$

As a consequence, d does not depend on f. Accordingly figure 4 graphs the verti-cal $\dot{d} = 0$ line.

Beyond that, equation (17) happens to be identical to equation (8). Differentiate equation (8) for f to accomplish:

$$\frac{\partial \dot{f}}{\partial f} = \frac{[(1-c)(m+b-g)-b]r}{(1-c+q)(m+b-g)-b} - n \tag{20}$$

To evaluate the sign of equation (20), it is useful to rewrite equation (5):

$$(1-c+q)(m+b-g)-b = e(j+rf) \tag{21}$$

In addition, set $\dot{f} = 0$ into equation (7):

$$(1-c)(m+b-g)-b = enf \tag{22}$$

Then substitute equations (21) and (22) into equation (20):

$$\frac{\partial \dot{f}}{\partial f} = -\frac{jn}{j+rf} \tag{23}$$

Due to $n > 0$, we achieve $\partial \dot{f} / \partial f < 0$. Last but not least, amalgamate $\dot{f} = 0$ and equation (8) to reach:

$$nf = \frac{[(1-c)(m+b-g)-b](j+rf)}{(1-c+q)(m+b-g)-b} \tag{24}$$

As a corollary, f is given irrespective of d. Figure 4 graphs the horizontal $\dot{f} = 0$ line. Fitting the puzzle together, the phase diagram demonstrates that the long-run equilibrium will be stable.

In summary, under exogenous fiscal policy, the long-run equilibrium will be stable. In this sense, exogenous fiscal policy can be sustained. Endogenous fiscal policy, however, is ineffective.

3. Summary

To begin with, we assume an economy without public sector. First consider the basic model. As a result, the long-run equilibrium will be stable. An increase in money supply per head in the short run raises output per head. Then, in the medium run, foreign assets per head start to accumulate. This in turn lowers output per head. In the long run, output per head does not fall below its initial level. An increase in investment per head in the short run has no effect on output per head. Then, in the medium run, foreign assets per head start to decline. Therefore output per head begins to grow. An increase in exports per head in the short run leaves no impact on output per head. Then, in the medium run, foreign assets per head do not move. That is why output per head does not move either. In this sense, a flexible exchange rate can be sustained.

Second regard endogenous monetary policy. The analysis yields a stability condition that empirically seems to be fulfilled. Take for instance a reduction in investment per head. In the short term, there is no need for a change in monetary policy. Then, in the intermediate term, foreign assets per head start to build up. To counteract this, the central bank must augment money supply per head. In this sense, endogenous monetary policy can be sustained.

Third imagine flexible money wages. There exists a stability condition that empirically seems to be sound. Take once more a reduction in investment per head. In the short run, prices do not respond. Then, in the medium run, foreign assets per head begin to accumulate. Owing to that, prices start to decline.

So far we assumed an economy without public sector. Now we shall introduce the public sector (and public debt). First have a look at exogenous fiscal policy. As a finding, the long-run equilibrium will be stable. Suppose that the government increases both its purchases per head and its deficit per head. In the short run, this does not affect output per head. Then, in the medium run, foreign assets per head come down. Due to that, output per head goes up. In this sense, exogenous fiscal policy can be sustained. Second take a glance at endogenous fiscal policy. As a conclusion, endogenous fiscal policy is plainly ineffective.

From the policy point of view, this can be summed up as follows. Fiscal policy is just ineffective. Monetary policy, on the other hand is effective. And what is more, it can be sustained. The reader may wish to consult table 27.

Table 27
Flexible Exchange Rate
Stability of Long-Run Equilibrium

basic model	stable
endogenous monetary policy	stable
flexible money wages	stable
exogenous fiscal policy	stable
endogenous fiscal policy	not feasible

Synopsis

First consider the stability of the long-run equilibrium in the open economy. For the basic model, the long-run equilibrium will be stable in any case. With endogenous exchange rate policy, this is somewhat different. Under a fixed exchange rate, the long-run equilibrium will be stable. But under a flexible exchange rate, endogenous exchange rate policy cannot be adopted. With endogenous monetary policy, it is the other way round. Under a fixed exchange rate, endogenous monetary policy cannot be implemented. But under a flexible exchange rate, the long-run equilibrium will be stable. For flexible money wages, the long-run equilibrium will be stable in any case. This holds for exogenous fiscal policy, too. With endogenous fiscal policy, this is quite different. Under a fixed exchange rate, the long-run equilibrium will be unstable. And under a flexible exchange rate, endogenous fiscal policy cannot be pursued. For a synopsis see table 28.

Table 28
Open Economy
Stability of Long-Run Equilibrium

	fixed exchange rate	flexible exchange rate
basic model	stable	stable
endogenous exchange rate policy	stable	not feasible
endogenous monetary policy	not feasible	stable
flexible money wages	stable	stable
exogenous fiscal policy	stable	stable
endogenous fiscal policy	unstable	not feasible

Second regard the sustainability of fiscal policy. Exogenous fiscal policy (i.e. a fixed deficit per head) can be sustained in any case. This applies to the closed economy as well as to the open economy. With endogenous fiscal policy, this is rather different. For the closed economy, this strategy can be sustained. Under a fixed exchange rate, however, it cannot be sustained. And under a flexible exchange rate, it is not feasible. Table 29 presents an overview.

Table 29
Sustainability of Fiscal Policy

	exogenous fiscal policy	endogenous fiscal policy
closed economy	sustainable	sustainable
fixed exchange rate	sustainable	not sustainable
flexible exchange rate	sustainable	not feasible

Third, what is the best endogenous policy, given a permanent shock? For the closed economy, it is monetary policy. Under a fixed exchange rate, it is exchange rate policy. And under a flexible exchange rate, we are back at monetary policy. The reader may wish to refer to table 30.

Table 30
Best Endogenous Policy (Permanent Shock)

closed economy	monetary policy
fixed exchange rate	exchange rate policy
flexible exchange rate	monetary policy

Conclusion

Let us begin with the closed economy (part I). The government can choose one out of three strategies. It can fix the deficit per head (section 1), the tax per head (section 2), or the tax rate (section 3). In section 1.1. we assume that the government fixes the deficit per head and that fiscal policy is exogenous. When the government fixes the deficit per head, then according to the budget identity it must adjust the tax per head. The analysis has been conducted within the framework of an IS growth model. Labour supply in terms of efficiency units grows at a constant rate.

The government raises loans and levies a tax in order to finance its purchases of goods and services as well as the interest payments on public debt. The government fixes both its purchases and its deficit on a per capita basis. The budget deficit in turn adds to public debt. Disposable income can be defined as the sum of factor income and public interest, net after tax respectively. Households consume a fixed share of disposable income. Firms fix investment on a per capita basis. And output is determined by aggregate demand.

In a growing economy, as an important result, the long-run equilibrium will be stable. In a stationary economy, however, the long-run equilibrium will be unstable. Henceforth we assume a growing economy. What are the key characteristics of the long-run equilibrium? An increase in investment per head raises output per head. It has no effects on public debt per head and the tax per head. An increase in government purchases per head raises output per head, too. Public debt per head stays constant, and the tax per head goes up. An increase in the budget deficit per head enhances output per head, public debt per head and the tax per head. An increase in the growth rate leaves no impact on output per head. It lowers public debt per head and the tax per head.

Finally have a look at the process of adjustment induced by a fiscal expansion. Initially the economy is in the long-run equilibrium. Government purchases per head, the budget deficit per head, public debt per head and the tax per head do not move. Output per head and consumption per head are invariant. Let the economy suffer from unemployment. Against this background, the government increases both its purchases per head and its deficit per head, by the same amount respectively. In the short run, this brings up output per head, thereby reducing unemployment. The tax per head does not respond, so consumption per head improves.

In the medium run, the increase in the budget deficit per head contributes to the accumulation of public debt per head. To cover the swell in public interest per head, the government must raise the tax per head. On balance, disposable income per head does not change. That is why consumption per head and output per head do not change either. As time passes away, the economy approaches a new long-run equilibrium. Public debt per head, the tax per head and output per head do not move any more. In summary, there is a one-time jump in output per head and consumption per head. Public debt per head and the tax per head have reached a higher level. In this sense, a fixed deficit per head can be sustained.

In section 1.3. fiscal policy becomes endogenous. As a response to a shock, the government continuously adjusts the budget deficit per head so as to maintain full employment all the time. In a growing economy, the long-run equilibrium will be stable.

Now we trace out the dynamics of a transitory investment shock. At the beginning, the economy is in the steady state. Suppose that each worker has got a job. Let the budget be balanced, so there is no public debt. The tax per head and output per head are uniform. In this situation, investment per head comes down. Instantaneously, to counteract this, the government increases the budget deficit per head. That is to say, the government reduces the tax per head, thus stimulating consumption per head. The net effect is that output per head does not change. Hence the labour market still clears. The increase in the budget deficit per head leads to the growth of public debt per head. To finance the expansion of public interest per head, the government must raise the tax per head.

After a certain span of time, let investment per head return to its original level. At once, therefore, the government reduces the budget deficit per head. Put another way, the government increases the tax per head, which curbs consumption per head. The reduction in the budget deficit per head leads to the decline of public debt per head. And the contraction of public interest per head allows the government to lower the tax per head. Asymptotically the economy converges to a new steady state. Full employment does always prevail. The budget is again balanced, and public debt has disappeared from the scene. The tax per head and output per head are uniform. In summary, all variables return to their initial levels. Public debt per head eliminates itself, even though the government does not switch to a budget surplus. The reason is that population growth (and technical progress) reduce public debt per head.

In section 2.1. we postulate that the government fixes the tax per head and that fiscal policy is exogenous. When the government fixes the tax per head, then according to the budget identity it must adjust the deficit per head. If the interest rate falls short of the growth rate, then the long-run equilibrium will be stable. Conversely, if the interest rate exceeds the growth rate, then the long-run equilibrium will be unstable. From the empirical point of view, the interest rate exceeds the growth rate, so the long-run equilibrium will be unstable.

Next we keep track of the process of adjustment occasioned by a fiscal expansion. At the start, the economy is in the long-run equilibrium without public debt. The budget is balanced, and output per head does not stir. Under these circumstances, the government increases its purchases per head, holding the tax per head constant. In the short run, this drives up output per head. And the budget gets into deficit. In the medium run, the budget deficit per head contributes to the accumulation of public debt per head. The swell in public interest per head augments disposable income per head, thereby promoting consumption per head and output per head. To finance the swell in public interest per head, the government must raise the deficit per head. This in turn speeds up the accumulation of public debt per head. In the long run, both public debt per head and output per head tend to explode. In this sense, a fixed tax per head cannot be sustained. This is in sharp contrast to a fixed deficit per head, which in fact can be sustained.

In section 2.2. fiscal policy becomes endogenous. The government period by period varies its purchases per head so as to defend full employment all the time. The investigation gives rise to a stability condition that empirically seems to be sound. Compare this to exogenous fiscal policy where the long-run equilibrium was unstable. Thus endogenous fiscal policy enhances (the likelihood of) stability. Take for instance a decline in investment per head. In the short run, leaning against the wind, the government increases its purchases per head. Then, in the medium run, public debt per head begins to build up. To compensate for this, the government reduces its purchases per head. And what is more, in the long run, government purchases per head fall below their initial level.

In section 3.1. we suppose that the government fixes the tax rate and that fiscal policy is exogenous. Strictly speaking, the government levies a proportionate tax on both factor income and public interest. The analysis yields a stability condition. Let this condition be fulfilled. First consider an increase in government purchases per head. In the short term, this policy measure boosts output per head. Then, in the intermediate term, public debt per head starts to grow. On that account, output per head continues to rise. Second regard an increase in investment per head. In the short term, this shock pushes up output per head. Then, in the intermediate term, public debt per head starts to decline. This in turn pulls down output per head. And in the long term, output per head falls below its original level.

Next we study the full dynamics of a fiscal expansion. At the outset, the economy is in the steady state without public debt. The budget is balanced, and output per head does not move. Against this background, the government increases its purchases per head, holding the tax rate constant. In the short term, this lifts output per head. And the budget changes into deficit.

In the intermediate term, the budget deficit per head contributes to the accumulation of public debt per head. The growth of public interest per head enlarges disposable income per head, thereby encouraging consumption per head and output per head. In addition, to cover public interest per head, the government must raise the deficit per head. Moreover, the growth of public interest per head and output per head augments tax revenue per head. In due course the economy approximates a new steady state. The budget deficit per head and public debt per head do not move any longer. The same applies to output per head. By the way, in the numerical example, the half-life of this process is about 80 years. Hence this is a very slow process. In summary, a fixed tax rate can possibly be sustained. This differs to a certain extent from a fixed tax per head, which cannot be sustained.

In section 3.2. fiscal policy becomes endogenous. The government continuously adjusts its purchases per head so as to safeguard full employment all the time. Upon closer inspection we get a stability condition. From the empirical point of view, this condition will be met.

At this point we leave the closed economy (part I) and come to the open economy (part II). The exchange rate can be either fixed (chapter I) or flexible (chapter II). Let us begin with a fixed exchange rate. In section 1 we have an economy without public sector. The investigation has been conducted within a small open economy characterized by perfect capital mobility. For the small open economy, the foreign interest rate is given exogenously. And under perfect capital mobility, the domestic interest rate agrees with the foreign interest rate. Therefore the domestic interest rate is constant, too.

Exports are fixed on a per capita basis. Domestic residents hold foreign assets and earn interest on them. The income of domestic residents consists of domestic income and the interest inflow. Imports are a certain fraction of the income of domestic residents. The current account surplus can be defined as the excess of exports and the interest inflow over imports. The current account surplus in turn adds to foreign assets. Consumption is a given share of the income of domestic residents. Investment is fixed on a per capita basis. And domestic output is governed by the demand for domestic goods.

The investigation gives rise to a stability condition. If the growth rate is high, then the long-run equilibrium will be stable. On the other hand, if the foreign interest rate is high, then the long-run equilibrium will be unstable. If the consumption rate is high, we are back at stability. And the same is true if the import rate is high. Empirical evidence seems to suggest that the long-run equilibrium will be stable.

What are the salient features of the long-run equilibrium? The high-exporting country will be a creditor, while the low-exporting country will be a debtor. The other way round, the high-investing country will be a debtor, while the low-investing country will be a creditor. Similarly the high-consuming country will be a debtor, whereas the low-consuming country will be a creditor. What is equivalent, the high-saving country will be a creditor, whereas the low-saving country will be a debtor. The high-importing country will be a debtor, while the low-importing country will be a creditor. If the foreign interest rate is high, then the country in question will be a creditor. But if the foreign interest rate is low, then the country will be a debtor.

Beyond that, an increase in exports per head causes an increase in foreign assets per head. An increase in investment per head, however, causes a reduction in foreign assets per head. Now imagine an increase in the growth rate. If the country is a creditor, then foreign assets per head decline. Conversely, if the country is a debtor, then it is foreign debt per head that declines.

What are the long-run implications for output per head? An increase in exports per head raises output per head. An increase in investment per head lowers output per head, which comes somehow as a surprise. Once more imagine an increase in the growth rate. If the country is a creditor, then output per head drops. But if the country is a debtor, then output per head climbs.

Next have a look at the process of adjustment. First consider an export shock. At the beginning, the economy is in the long-run equilibrium. Let the trade account, the current account and the foreign position be balanced. Output per head is invariant. In this situation, exports per head go up. In the short run, this enhances output per head. Both the trade account and the current account get into surplus.

In the medium run, the current account surplus per head contributes to the accumulation of foreign assets per head. The expansion of the interest inflow per head augments the income of domestic residents per head, thus stimulating consumption per head as well as output per head. Besides, the expansion of the interest inflow per head reinforces the current account surplus per head. Moreover the growth of the income of domestic residents per head brings up imports per head. This in turn cuts back the trade surplus per head. After a certain interval of time, the trade account changes into deficit. In the end, the economy gravitates towards a new long-run equilibrium. The motion of the current account surplus per head and of foreign assets per head comes to a halt. The same applies to the trade deficit per head and to output per head. The country in question has become a creditor. It runs a current account surplus and a trade deficit.

Second regard an investment shock. Initially the economy is in the steady state. Again let the trade account, the current account and the foreign position be balanced. Output per head is uniform. Under these circumstances, investment per head jumps up. In the short term, this lifts output per head. Imports per head mount, hence both the trade account and the current account get into deficit.

In the intermediate term, the current account deficit per head contributes to the accumulation of foreign debt per head. The swell of the interest outflow per head diminishes the income of domestic residents per head, in this way restraining consumption per head and output per head. Further the swell of the interest outflow per head elevates the current account deficit per head. Over and above that, the decline of the income of domestic residents per head puts downward pressure on imports per head. This in turn reduces the trade deficit per head. After some time, the trade account changes into surplus. Finally the economy tends to a new steady state. The current account deficit per head and foreign debt per head stop moving. The same holds for the trade surplus per head and for output per head. The country has become a debtor. It runs a current account deficit and a trade surplus.

In addition we address endogenous exchange rate policy. The government continuously varies the exchange rate so as to maintain full employment all the time. Closer examination reveals a stability condition that empirically seems to be safe. Imagine for instance a cut in investment per head. In the short run, to prevent unemployment from coming into existence, the government pushes up the exchange rate (i.e. it devalues domestic currency). Then, in the medium run, foreign assets per head start to pile up. To offset this, the government pulls down the exchange rate (i.e. it revalues domestic currency). And in the long run, the exchange rate is fixed below its original level.

In section 2, the public sector (and public debt) are incorporated into the model. The government fixes its purchases of goods and services on a per capita basis. Likewise the government fixes its deficit on a per capita basis. The budget deficit in turn adds to public debt. The government pays interest on its debt. The disposable income of domestic residents can be defined as the sum of domestic income, the interest inflow and public interest, net after tax respectively. Imports are a certain fraction of the disposable income of domestic residents. The current account surplus can be defined as the excess of exports and the interest inflow over imports. The current account surplus in turn adds to foreign assets. The analysis delivers a stability condition that from the empirical point of view will be fulfilled.

What are the principal attributes of the long-run equilibrium? The high budget deficit country will be a debtor. It registers a current account deficit and a trade surplus. The low budget deficit country, on the other hand, will be a creditor. It experiences a current account surplus and a trade deficit. Consider for example a simultaneous increase in government purchases per head and the budget deficit per head, by the same amount respectively. This policy measure increases public debt per head and reduces foreign assets per head. More precisely, the reduction in foreign assets per head is greater than the increase in public debt per head. As a consequence, on balance, output per head comes down.

Now we trace out the process of adjustment induced by a fiscal expansion. At the beginning, the economy is in the long-run equilibrium. Let the budget be balanced, so there exists no public debt. Similarly let the trade account, the current account and the foreign position be balanced. Output per head is constant. Against this background, the government raises both its purchases per head and its deficit per head. In the short run, this drives up output per head. The budget gets into deficit. Imports per head go up, so the trade account and the current account get into deficit as well.

In the medium run, the budget deficit per head contributes to the accumulation of public debt per head. At the same time, the current account deficit per head contributes to the accumulation of foreign debt per head. The surge in the interest outflow per head diminishes the income of domestic residents per head. This in turn brings down consumption per head and hence output per head. Besides, the diminution of the income of domestic residents per head depresses imports per head and thus the trade deficit per head. After a certain span of time, the trade account changes into surplus.

With the lapse of time, the economy approaches a new long-run equilibrium. The budget deficit per head and public debt per head cease to move. The same is true of the current account deficit per head and foreign debt per head. Output per head is again constant. Properly speaking, foreign debt per head exceeds public debt per head. And the current account deficit per head surpasses the budget deficit per head. What is more, output per head has settled down well below its initial level. From the policy point of view, this can be rephrased as follows. In the short run, fiscal policy reduces unemployment. In the long run, however, it increases unemployment. This seems to be an important result.

Next we proceed from exogenous to endogenous fiscal policy. The government continuously varies its purchases per head and its deficit per head so as to defend full employment all the time. As a finding, the long-term equilibrium will be unstable. This clearly differs from the conclusions drawn for exogenous fiscal policy.

To illustrate this, we keep track of the transitional dynamics generated by a permanent export shock. Originally the economy is in the steady state. Let the budget be balanced, so there exists no public debt. And let the current account be balanced, so the foreign position is balanced, too. Output per head is uniform. In this situation, exports per head drop. In the short term, to counteract this, the government lifts both its purchases per head and its deficit per head. The net effect is that output per head does not stir. Each worker has still got a job.

In the intermediate term, the current account deficit per head leads to the growth of foreign debt per head. And the budget deficit per head leads to the growth of public debt per head. The expansion of the interest outflow per head contracts the income of domestic residents per head, thereby restraining consumption per head. To ward off unemployment, the government continues to lift its purchases per head and its deficit per head. In the long term, foreign debt per head grows without limits. And much the same applies to public debt per head. To sum up, endogenous fiscal policy is effective in the short term, but it cannot be sustained.

In chapter II we leave the fixed exchange rate and turn to a flexible exchange rate. In section 1, we have an economy without public sector. Exports per head are an increasing function of the exchange rate. Money demand is an increasing function of the income of domestic residents. The central bank fixes money supply on a per capita basis. In equilibrium, money supply harmonizes with money demand. In a growing economy, as an outcome, the long-run equilibrium will be stable. In a stationary economy, the other way round, the long-run equilibrium will be unstable. We still regard a growing economy.

What are the main properties of the long-run equilibrium? The high-liquidity country (i.e. the country marked by a big money supply per head) will be a creditor, whereas the low-liquidity country will be a debtor. The high-investing country will be a debtor, whereas the low-investing country will be a creditor. Analogously, the high-consuming country will be a debtor, while the low-consuming country will be a creditor. What is identical, the high-saving country will be a creditor, while the low-saving country will be a debtor.

Beyond that, an increase in money supply per head causes an increase in foreign assets per head. An increase in investment per head causes a reduction in foreign assets per head. And an increase in exports per head has no influence upon foreign assets per head. Further imagine an increase in the growth rate. If the country in question is a creditor, then foreign assets per head decline. Conversely, if the country is a debtor, then it is foreign debt per head that declines.

What are the long-run implications for output per head? An increase in money supply per head raises output per head. The same is true of an increase in investment per head. And an increase in exports per head does not affect output per head. Once more imagine an increase in the growth rate. If the country is a creditor, then output per head rises. Conversely, if the country is a debtor, then output per head falls.

Next have a look at the process of adjustment. First consider a monetary expansion. At the beginning, the economy is in the long-run equilibrium. Let the trade account, the current account and the foreign position be balanced. Output per head is constant. Against this background, the central bank augments money supply per head. In the short run, as a response, domestic currency depreciates. This in turn advances exports per head and output per head. The trade account gets into surplus, as does the current account.

In the medium run, the current account surplus per head contributes to the accumulation of foreign assets per head. For that reason, domestic currency appreciates. This on its part curbs exports per head and output per head. Besides, the contraction of exports per head cuts back the trade surplus per head. After a certain interval of time, the trade account changes into deficit. In the end, the economy tends to a new long-run equilibrium. The motion of the current account surplus per head and of foreign assets per head comes to a standstill. The same holds for the trade deficit per head. Output per head is again constant. To sum up, the country has become a creditor. It runs a current account surplus and a trade deficit. Output per head lies well above its initial level.

Second regard an investment shock. Originally the economy is in the steady state. Let the trade account, the current account and the foreign position be balanced. Output per head is invariant. In this situation, investment per head springs up. In the short term, owing to that, domestic currency appreciates. This in turn puts a brake upon exports per head. The net effect is that output per head does not move. Both the trade account and the current account get into deficit.

In the intermediate term, the current account deficit per head leads to the growth of foreign debt per head. Due to that, domestic currency depreciates. This on its part promotes exports per head and output per head. Moreover the increase in exports per head reduces the trade deficit per head. After some time, the trade account changes into surplus. Asymptotically the economy converges to a new steady state. The current account deficit per head and foreign debt per head do not adjust any longer. The same applies to the trade surplus per head. Output per head is again invariant. The country has become a debtor. It runs a current account deficit and a trade surplus.

Last but not least take a glance at endogenous monetary policy. The central bank continuously varies money supply per head so as to safeguard full employment all the time. The investigation provides a stability condition that empirically seems to be sound. Imagine for instance a reduction in investment per head. In the short run, there is no need for the central bank to step in. Then, in the medium run, foreign assets per head start to build up. To offset this, the central bank augments money supply per head.

In section 2, the public sector (and public debt) enter the model. As an outcome, the long-run equilibrium proves to be stable. What are the key characteristics of the long-run equilibrium? The high budget deficit country will be a debtor, whereas the low budget deficit country will be a creditor. Consider a simultaneous increase in government purchases per head and the budget deficit per head, by the same amount respectively. This policy measure raises public debt per head and lowers foreign assets per head. Strictly speaking, the reduction in foreign assets is equal in size to the increase in public debt per head. Over and above that, the policy measure brings up output per head.

To elucidate this, we discuss the dynamic consequences of a fiscal impulse. At the outset, the economy is in the long-run equilibrium. Let the budget be balanced, so there exists no public debt. Likewise let the trade account, the current account and the foreign position be balanced. Output per head is uniform. Under these circumstances, the government boosts its purchases per head and its deficit per head. In the short run, as a reaction, domestic currency appreciates. This in turn impedes exports per head. Therefore, on balance, output per head remains unchanged. The budget gets into deficit. The same is true of the trade account and the current account.

In the medium run, the budget deficit per head contributes to the accumulation of public debt per head. Similarly the current account deficit per head contributes to the accumulation of foreign debt per head. On these grounds, domestic currency depreciates. This on its part stimulates exports per head and output per head. Further the growth of exports per head diminishes the trade deficit per head. After some time, the trade account changes into surplus. Ultimately the economy reaches a new long-run equilibrium. The budget deficit per head and public debt per head stop moving. Much the same holds for the current account deficit per head and foreign debt per head. More exactly, public debt per head and foreign debt per head are the same size. Analogously, the budget deficit per head and the current account deficit per head are the same size. So much for exogenous fiscal policy. Endogenous fiscal policy is ineffective, as can easily be seen.

Result

Let us begin with the closed economy. First consider a fixed deficit per head. If the government fixes the deficit per head, then according to the budget identity it must adjust the tax per head. In a growing economy, the long-run equilibrium will be stable. In a stationary economy, on the other hand, the long-run equilibrium will be unstable. Henceforth we assume a growing economy. Take for instance a simultaneous increase in government purchases per head and the budget deficit per head. In the short run, this raises output per head. Then, in the medium run, public debt per head and the tax per head start to grow. Output per head, however, does not move any longer. Put another way, there is a one-time jump in output per head. In this sense, a fixed deficit per head can be sustained.

Second regard a fixed tax per head. When the government fixes the tax per head, then according to the budget identity it must adjust the deficit per head. The analysis yields a stability condition. If the interest rate falls short of the growth rate, the long-run equilibrium will be stable. Conversely, if the interest rate exceeds the growth rate, the long-run equilibrium will be unstable. From the empirical point of view, the interest rate surpasses the growth rate, so the long-run equilibrium will in fact be unstable. Take for instance an increase in government purchases per head, holding the tax per head constant. In the short run, this brings up output per head. Then, in the medium run, public debt per head begins to accumulate. That is why output per head continues to rise. In the long run, both public debt per head and output per head tend to explode. In this sense, a fixed tax per head cannot be sustained.

Third imagine a fixed tax rate. Under this strategy, there exists a stability condition that empirically seems to be open to question. For the moment let this condition be fulfilled. Take for instance an increase in government purchases per head, holding the tax rate constant. In the short run, as a response, output per head goes up. Then, in the medium run, public debt per head starts to grow. Therefore output per head keeps on going up. In this sense, a fixed tax rate can possibly be sustained.

We come now to the open economy. First consider a fixed exchange rate. In addition we suppose that the government fixes the budget deficit per head. The analysis provides a stability condition that empirically seems to be met. An increase in exports per head in the short run pushes up output per head. Then, in the medium run, foreign assets per head begin to accumulate. By virtue of that, output per head continues to expand. An increase in investment per head in the short run augments output per head. Then, in the medium run, foreign assets per head start to decumulate. This in turn diminishes output per head. And in the long run, output per head falls below its initial level. A simultaneous increase in government purchases per head and the budget deficit per head in the short run drives up output per head. Then, in the medium run, foreign assets per head begin to decline. Owing to that, output per head is cut back. And in the long run, output per head is reduced below its original level.

Second regard a flexible exchange rate. In a growing economy, the long-run equilibrium will be stable. In a stationary economy, the other way round, the long-run equilibrium will be unstable. We still assume a growing economy. An increase in money supply per head in the short run raises output per head. Then, in the medium run, foreign assets per head start to build up. This in turn lowers output per head. But in the long run, output per head stays above its initial level. An increase in investment per head in the short run leaves no impact on output per head. Then, in the medium run, foreign assets per head begin to decline. Due to that, output per head starts to grow. An increase in exports per head in the short run has no effect on output per head. Then, in the medium run, foreign assets per head do not move either way. That is why output per head remains fixed. A simultaneous increase in government purchases per head and the budget deficit per head in the short run does not impinge on output per head. Then, in the medium run, foreign assets per head begin to decumulate. Therefore output per head starts to go up.

Next have a look at endogenous fiscal policy. As a response to a shock, the government continuously adjusts its purchases per head and its deficit per head so as to maintain full employment all the time. In the closed economy, this strategy is effective in the short run. And what is more, it can be sustained. Under a fixed exchange rate, this strategy is effective in the short run. However, it cannot be sustained. Under a flexible exchange rate, this strategy is ineffective even in the short run.

Similarly take a glance at endogenous monetary policy. The central bank continuously adjusts money supply per head so as to defend full employment all the time. In the closed economy, this strategy is effective in the short run. Beyond that, it can be sustained. Under a fixed exchange rate, this strategy is ineffective even in the short run. Under a flexible exchange rate, this strategy is effective in the short run. Over and above that, it can be sustained.

Finally, what is the best endogenous policy? In the closed economy, endogenous monetary policy bears the palm. Under a fixed exchange rate, the winner is endogenous exchange rate policy. And under a flexible exchange rate, we are back at endogenous monetary policy.

Symbols

A	assets, wealth
B	budget deficit, domestic bonds
C	(private) consumption
D	public debt
F	foreign assets, foreign bonds
G	government purchases of goods and services
H	trade surplus
I	(private) investment
K	(private) capital
L	money demand, labour demand
M	money supply
N	labour supply
Q	imports
R	reserves (foreign exchange)
S	(private) savings
T	tax
X	exports
Y	(domestic) output, income
Z	current account surplus

a	assets, wealth per head
b	budget deficit per head, domestic bonds per head
c	(marginal) consumption rate
cc	consumption per head
d	public debt per head
e	exchange rate
f	foreign assets per head, foreign bonds per head
g	government purchases per head
h	trade surplus per head
i	investment per head
j	exchange rate sensitivity
k	capital per head

m	money supply per head
n	growth rate of labour supply
p	price of domestic goods
p*	price of foreign goods
q	import rate
qq	imports per head
r	interest rate
s	savings per head
t	tax rate, tax per head
u	time
v	capital-output ratio
w	g - b
x	exports per head
y	output per head, income per head
z	current account surplus per head

α	wealth sensitivity of consumption
γ	interest sensitivity of investment, current account deficit per head
δ	interest sensitivity of money demand, foreign debt per head
ε	function
η	function
κ	income sensitivity of money demand
λ	speed of adjustment
μ	critical value, speed of adjustment
π	productivity

References

ALLEN, P. R., Financing Budget Deficits, in: European Economic Review 10, 1977, 345 - 373

ALLEN, P. R., A Portfolio Approach to International Capital Flows, in: Journal of International Economics 3, 1973, 135 - 160

ALLEN, P. R., KENEN, P. B., Asset Markets, Exchange Rates and Economic Integration, Cambridge 1980

ALLEN, P. R., KENEN., P. B., Portfolio Adjustment in Open Economies, in: Weltwirtschaftliches Archiv 112, 1976, 33 - 72

AOKI, M., Dynamic Analysis of Open Economies, New York 1981

ARGY, V., International Macroeconomics, London 1994

ARROW, K. J., BOSKIN, M. J., Eds., The Economics of Public Debt, New York 1988

ARTIS, M., Recent Developments in the Theory of Fiscal Policy, in: S. T. Cook, P. M. Jackson, Eds., Current Issues in Fiscal Policy, Oxford 1979

ATKINSON, A. B., STIGLITZ, J. E., Lectures on Public Economics, London 1980

AUERBACH, A. J., FELDSTEIN, M., Eds., Handbook of Public Economics, Amsterdam 1987

AUERBACH, A. J., KOTLIKOFF, L. J., Dynamic Fiscal Policy, Cambridge 1987

AZARIADIS, C., Intertemporal Macroeconomics, Oxford 1993

BARRO, R. J., Are Government Bonds Net Wealth?, in: Journal of Political Economy 82, 1974, 1095 - 1117

BARRO, R. J., SALA-I-MARTIN, X., Public Finance in Models of Economic Growth, in: Review of Economic Studies 59, 1992, 645 - 661

BARTH, J. R., et al, The Efficacy of Bond-Financed Fiscal Policy, in: Public Finance Quarterly 8, 1980, 323 - 344

BARTH, J. R., IDEN, G. R., RUSSEK, F. S., The Economic Consequences of Federal Deficits, in: Southern Economic Journal 52, 1986, 27 - 50

BARTH, J. R., IDEN, G. R., RUSSEK, F. S., Government Debt, Government Spending and Private Sector Behaviour: Comment, in: American Economic Review 76, 1986, 1158 - 1167

BARTSCH, P., Zur Theorie der längerfristigen Wirkungen "expansiver" Fiskalpolitik, Frankfurt 1986

BLANCHARD, O., Is There a Core of Usable Macroeconomics?, in: American Economic Review, Papers and Proceedings 87, 1997, 244 - 246

BLANCHARD, O., CHOURAQUI, J., HAGEMAN, R., SARTOR, N., The Sustainability of Fiscal Policy: New Answers to Old Questions, in: OECD Economic Studies 15, 1990, 7 - 36

BLANCHARD, O., DORNBUSCH, R., BUITER, W., Public Debt and Fiscal Responsibility, in: O. Blanchard, R. Dornbusch, R. Layard, Eds., Restoring Europe's Prosperity, Cambridge 1986

BLANCHARD, O., DORNBUSCH, R., LAYARD, R., Eds., Restoring Europe's Prosperity, Cambridge 1986

BLANCHARD, O. J., FISCHER, S., Lectures on Macroeconomics, Cambridge 1989

BLINDER, A. S., Is There a Core of Practical Macroeconomics That We Should All Believe?, in: American Economic Review, Papers and Proceedings 87, 1997, 240 - 243

BLINDER, A. S., SOLOW, R. M., Analytical Foundations of Fiscal Policy, in: A. S. Blinder, R. M. Solow, Eds., The Economics of Public Finance, Washington 1974

BLINDER, A. S., SOLOW, R. M., Does Fiscal Policy Matter?, in: Journal of Public Economics 2, 1973, 319 - 337

BLINDER, A. S., SOLOW, R. M., Does Fiscal Policy Matter? A Correction, in: Journal of Public Economics 5, 1976, 183 - 184

BLINDER, A. S., SOLOW, R. M., Does Fiscal Policy Still Matter? A Reply, in: Journal of Monetary Economics 2, 1976, 501 - 510

BLINDER, A. S., SOLOW, R. M. et al., Eds., The Economics of Public Finance, Washington 1974

BOSKIN, M. J., FLEMMING, J. S., GORINI, S., Eds., Private Saving and Public Debt, Oxford 1987

BOYER, R. S., Devaluation and Portfolio Balance, in: American Economic Review 67, 1977, 54 - 63

BOYER, R. S., Financial Policies in an Open Economy, in: Economica 45, 1978, 39 - 57

BRANSON, W. H., Asset Markets and Relative Prices in Exchange Rate Determination, in: Sozialwissenschaftliche Annalen 1, 1977, 69 - 89

BRANSON, W. H., The Dual Roles of the Government Budget and the Balance of Payments in the Movement from Short-Run to Long-Run Equilibrium, in: Quarterly Journal of Economics 90, 1976, 345 - 367

BRANSON, W. H., Exchange Rate Dynamics and Monetary Policy, in: A. Lindbeck, Ed., Inflation and Employment in Open Economies, Amsterdam 1979

BRANSON, W. H., Monetary Policy and the New View of International Capital Movements, in: Brookings Papers on Economic Activity 2, 1970, 235 - 262

BRANSON, W., BUITER, W., Monetary and Fiscal Policy With Flexible Exchange Rates, in: J. S. Bhandari, B. H. Putnam, Eds., Economic Interdependence and Flexible Exchange Rates, Cambridge 1983

BRANSON, W. H., HENDERSON, D. W., The Specification and Influence of Asset Markets, in: R. W. Jones, P. B. Kenen, Eds., Handbook of International Economics, Amsterdam 1985

BRÄUNINGER, M., Rentenversicherung und Kapitalbildung, Heidelberg 1998

BRUCE, N., The IS-LM Model of Macroeconomic Equilibrium and the Monetarist Controversy, in: Journal of Political Economy 85, 1977, 1049 - 1062

BRUNNER, K., MELTZER, A. H., An Aggregative Theory for a Closed Economy, in: J. L. Stein, Ed., Monetarism, Amsterdam 1976

BUITER, W. H., A Guide to Public Sector Debt and Deficits, in: Economic Policy 1, 1985, 13 - 79

BUITER, W. H., International Macroeconomics, Oxford 1990

BUITER, W. H., Principles of Budgetary and Financial Policy, Cambridge 1990

BUITER, W. H., Short-Run and Long-Run Effects of External Disturbances Under Floating Exchange Rate, in: Economica 45, 1978, 251 - 272

BUITER, W. H., Temporary Equilibrium and Long-Run Equilibrium, New York 1979

BUITER, W. H., Time Preference and International Lending and Borrowing in an Overlapping Generations Model, in: Journal of Political Economy 89, 1981, 769 - 797

BURDA, M., WYPLOSZ, C., Macroeconomics, Oxford 1997

BUTKIEWICZ, J. L., On Fiscal Policy and Macroeconomic Stability, in: Public Finance Quarterly 10, 1982, 39 - 47

CANSIER, D., Vermögenseffekte der Staatsverschuldung, in: Kredit und Kapital 14, 1981, 390 - 411

CARLBERG, M., Deutsche Vereinigung, Kapitalbildung und Beschäftigung, Heidelberg 1996

CARLBERG, M., International Economic Growth, Heidelberg 1997

CARLBERG, M., Makroökonomik der offenen Wirtschaft, München 1989

CARLBERG, M., Monetary and Fiscal Dynamics, New York 1992

CARLBERG, M., Open Economy Dynamics, New York 1993

CARLBERG, M., Sustainability and Optimality of Public Debt, Heidelberg 1995

CEBULA, R. J., IS-LM Stability and Economic Policy Effectiveness, in: Journal of Macroeconomics 2, 1980, 181 - 183

CHIANG, A. C., Elements of Dynamic Optimization, New York 1992

CHRIST, C. F., Some Dynamic Theory of Macroeconomic Policy Effects on Income and Prices under the Government Budget Restraint, in: Journal of Monetary Economics 4, 1978, 45 - 70

CHRIST, C. F., On Fiscal and Monetary Policies and the Government Budget Restraint, in: American Economic Review 69, 1979, 526 - 538

CLAASSEN, E. M., Global Monetary Economics, Oxford 1996

COHEN, D., DE LEEUW, F., A Note on the Government Budget Restraint, in: Journal of Monetary Economics 6, 1980, 547 - 560

CURRIE, D. A., Fiscal Policy and Stability in a Dynamic Macroeconomic Model with a Government Budget Restraint - A Comment, in: Public Finance 32, 1977, 412 - 417

CURRIE, D. A., Macroeconomic Policy and Government Financing, in: M. J. Artis, A. R. Nobay, Eds., Contemporary Economic Analysis, London 1978

CURRIE, D. A., Optimal Stabilization Policies and the Government Budget Constraint, in: Economica 43, 1976, 159 - 167

DIAMOND, P. A., National Debt in a Neoclassical Growth Model, in: American Economic Review 55, 1965, 1126 - 1150

DOMAR, E. D., The "Burden of the Debt" and the National Income, in: American Economic Review 34, 1944, 798 - 827

DOMAR, E. D., The Effect of Foreign Investment on the Balance of Payments, in: American Economic Review 40, 1950, 805 - 826

DORNBUSCH, R., Open Economy Macroeconomics, New York 1980

DORNBUSCH, R., Real Exchange Rates and Macroeconomics: A Selective Survey, in: S. Honkapohja, Ed., The State of Macroeconomics, Oxford 1990

DORNBUSCH, R., GIOVANNINI, A., Monetary Policy in the Open Economy, in: B. M. Friedman, F. H. Hahn, Eds., Handbook of Monetary Economics, Amsterdam 1990

ELTIS, W., Some Implications of Deficit-Financed Tax Cuts: These Will Always Increase Demand, but Will They Reduce Supply?, in: M. J. Boskin, J. S. Flemming, S. Gorini, Eds., Private Saving and Public Debt, Oxford 1987

FARMER, K., WENDNER, R., Wachstum und Außenhandel, Heidelberg 1997

FLASCHEL, P., FRANKE, R., SEMMLER, W., Dynamic Macroeconomics, Cambridge 1997

FLASCHEL, P., GROH, G., Keynesianische Makroökonomik, Berlin 1996

FLEMING, J. M., Domestic Financial Policies under Fixed and Floating Exchange Rates, in: IMF Staff Papers 9, 1962, 369 - 380

FRENKEL, J. A., MUSSA, M. L., Asset Markets, Exchange Rates and the Balance of Payments, in: R. W. Jones, P. B. Kenen, Eds., Handbook of International Economics, Amsterdam 1985

FRENKEL, J. A., RAZIN, A., Fiscal Policies and Growth in the World Economy, Cambridge 1996

FRENKEL, J. A., RAZIN, A., Fiscal Policies and the World Economy, Cambridge 1992

FRENKEL, J., RAZIN, A., The Mundell-Fleming Model a Quarter Century Later, in: IMF Staff Papers 34, 1987, 567 - 620

FRENKEL, J. A., RODRIGUEZ, C. A., Portfolio Equilibrium and the Balance of Payments: A Monetary Approach, in: American Economic Review 65, 1975, 674 - 688

FRIEDMAN, B. M., HAHN, F. H., Eds., Handbook of Monetary Economics, Amsterdam 1990

FRIEDMAN, M., A Monetary and Fiscal Framework for Economic Stability, in: American Economic Review 38, 1948, 245 - 264

GAHLEN, B., HESSE, H., RAMSER, H. J., Hg., Finanzmärkte, Tübingen 1997

GALE, D., Money: In Disequilibrium, Cambridge 1983

GANDOLFO, G., Economic Dynamics, Berlin 1997

GANDOLFO, G., International Economics, Berlin 1995

GRÖSSL-GSCHWENDTNER, I., Wirkungen staatlicher Budgetdefizite, Tübingen 1990

GROSSMAN, G. M., ROGOFF, K., Eds., Handbook of International Economics, Amsterdam 1995

HALIASSOS, M., TOBIN, J., The Macroeconomics of Government Finance, in: B. M. Friedman, F. H. Hahn, Eds., Handbook of Monetary Economics, Amsterdam 1990

HAMADA, K., Economic Growth and Long-Term International Capital Movements, in: Yale Economic Essays 6, 1966, 49 - 96

HAYAKAWA, H., Does Fiscal Policy Really Matter in the Context of Variable Prices?, in: Journal of Macroeconomics 1, 1979, 321 - 346

INFANTE, E. F., STEIN, J. L., Does Fiscal Policy Matter?, in: Journal of Monetary Economics 2, 1976, 473 - 500

JAEGER, K., Diskrete und stetige Analyse im IS-LM Modell, in: Zeitschrift für die gesamte Staatswissenschaft 139, 1983, 229 - 244

JONES, R. W., KENEN, P. B., Eds., Handbook of International Economics, Amsterdam 1985

KATSELI-PAPAEFSTRATIOU, L. T., MARION, N. P., Adjustment to Variations in Imported Input Prices, in: National Bureau of Economic Research, Working Paper 501, 1980

KATZ, E., A Note on Bond Finance, Perfect Capital Mobility, and Stability, in: Oxford Economic Papers 29, 1977, 141 - 144

KENEN, P. B., The International Economy, Cambridge 1994

KLAUSINGER, H., Zur dynamischen Makro-Theorie einer offenen Wirtschaft, in: J. H. Pichler, Hg., Strategien der Wechselkurspolitik, Berlin 1986

KRUGMAN, P. R., OBSTFELD, M., International Economics, New York 1994

LACHMANN, W., Fiskalpolitik, Berlin 1987

LICHTENAUER, P., Konsolidierung des Budgets, Abbau der Staatsschulden und Kapitalbildung, Frankfurt 1997

MANKIW, N. G., Macroeconomic Consequences of Government Debt, in: J. B. Taylor, M. Woodford, Eds., Handbook of Macroeconomics, Amsterdam (forthcoming)

MAUSSNER, A., KLUMP, R., Wachstumstheorie, Berlin 1996

MCCALLUM, B. T., Are Bond-Financed Deficits Inflationary?, in: Journal of Political Economy 92, 1984, 123 - 135

MCCALLUM, B. T., International Monetary Economics, New York 1996

MCGRATH, B., Implications of the Government Budget Constraint, in: Journal of Money, Credit and Banking 9, 1977, 304 - 315

MCKINNON, R. I., OATES, W. E., The Implications of International Economic Integration for Monetary, Fiscal and Exchange-Rate Policy, in: Princeton Studies in International Finance 16, 1966

MICHAELIS, J., Zur Ökonomie von Entlohnungssystemen, Tübingen 1998

MILLER, S. M., Dynamic Monetary and Fiscal Policy and the Government Budget Restraint: A Growth Equilibrium, in: Journal of Macroeconomics 2, 1980, 199 - 212

MITCHELL, D. W., The Feasibility of Perpetual Deficits, in: Journal of Macroeconomics 10, 1988, 407 - 419

MODIGLIANI, F., ANDO, A., Impacts of Fiscal Actions on Aggregate Income and the Monetarist Controversy: Theory and Evidence, in: J. L. Stein, Ed., Monetarism, Amsterdam 1976

MÜCKL, W. J., Ein Beitrag zur Theorie der Staatsverschuldung, in: Finanzarchiv 39, 1981, 253 - 278

MUNDELL, R. A., International Economics, New York 1968

MUSGRAVE, R. A., Reconsidering the Fiscal Role of Government, in: American Economic Review, Papers and Proceedings 87, 1997, 156 - 159

NIEHANS, J., A Comment on Stabilization Paradoxes, in: H. Albach, Ed., Quantitative Wirtschaftsforschung, Tübingen 1977

NIEHANS, J., Geschichte der Außenwirtschaftstheorie im Überblick, Tübingen 1995

OATES, W. E., Budget Balance and Equilibrium Income: A Comment on the Efficacy of Fiscal and Monetary Policy in an Open Economy, in: Journal of Finance 21, 1966, 489 - 498

OBSTFELD, M., ROGOFF, K., Foundations of International Macroeconomics, Cambridge 1996

O'CONNELL, S. A., ZELDES, S. P., Rational Ponzi Games, in: International Economic Review 29, 1988, 431 - 450

OHR, R., Budgetpolitik in offenen Volkswirtschaften, Berlin 1987

OTT, D. J., OTT, A. F., Budget Balance and Equilibrium Income, in: Journal of Finance 20, 1965, 71 - 77

PAPADOPOULOU, D. M., Makroökonomik der Wechselkursunion, Frankfurt 1993

PERSSON, T., Global Effects of National Stabilization Policies under Fixed and Floating Exchange Rates, in: Scandinavian Journal of Economics 84, 1982, 165 - 192

PFÄHLER, W., Kurz-, mittel- und langfristige Effekte der Fiskalpolitik in diskreter Analyse, in: Finanzarchiv 40, 1982, 281 - 305

PHELPS, E. S., SHELL, K., Public Debt, Taxation and Capital Intensiveness, in: Journal of Economic Theory 1, 1969, 330 - 346

PHELPS, E. S., VELUPILLAI, K., Optimum Fiscal Policy when Monetary Policy is Bound by a Rule: Ramsey Redux, in: K. J. Arrow, M. J. Boskin, Eds., The Economics of Public Debt, New York 1988

VAN DER PLOEG, F., Ed., Handbook of International Macroeconomics, Oxford 1994

POSSEN, U. M., The Long-Run Properties of an Income-Expenditure Model, in: Economica 46, 1979, 159 - 173

RAU, N., Simplifying the Theory of the Government Budget Restraint, in: Oxford Economic Papers 37, 1985, 210 - 229

RODRIGUEZ, C. A., Short- and Long-Run Effects of Monetary and Fiscal Policies Under Flexible Exchange Rates and Perfect Capital Mobility, in: American Economic Review 69, 1979, 176 - 182

SAMUELSON, P. A., Interactions between the Multiplier Analysis and the Principle of Acceleration, in: Review of Economics and Statistics 21, 1939, 75 - 78

SARGENT, T. J., Macroeconomic Theory, Boston 1987

SARGENT, T. J., WALLACE, N., Some Unpleasant Monetarist Arithmetic, in: Federal Reserve Board of Minneapolis Quarterly Review 5, 1981, 1 - 17

SAUERNHEIMER, K., Internationale Kapitalbewegungen, flexible Wechselkurse und gesamtwirtschaftliches Gleichgewicht, Hamburg 1980

SCARTH, W. M., Bond-Financed Fiscal Policy and the Problem of Instrument Instability, in: Journal of Macroeconomics 1, 1979, 107 - 117

SCARTH, W. M., Can Economic Growth Make Monetarist Arithmetic Pleasant?, in: Southern Economic Journal 53, 1987, 1028 - 1036

SCARTH, W. M., Fiscal Policy and the Government Budget Constraint under Alternative Exchange-Rate Systems, in: Oxford Economic Papers 27, 1975, 10 - 20

SCARTH, W. M., The Government Budget Constraint in an Open Economy: A Further Comment, in: Oxford Economic Papers 29, 1977, 145 - 151

SCARTH, W. M., A Note on the "Crowding Out" of Private Expenditures by Bond Financed Increases in Government Spending, in: Journal of Public Economics 5, 1976, 385 - 387

SHIEH, Y. N., The Efficacy of Bond-Financed Fiscal Policy, in: Public Finance Quarterly 10, 1982, 119 - 125

SHIEH, Y. N., A Note on Bond Finance and Stability in a Simple Income-Expenditure Model, in: Public Finance 35, 1980, 464 - 473

SHONE, R., Economic Dynamics, Cambridge 1997

SIEBKE, J., KNOLL, D., SCHMIDBERGER, W. D., Theoretische Grundlagen des crowding-out-Effektes, in: W. Ehrlicher, Hg., Geldpolitik, Zins und Staatsverschuldung, Berlin 1981

SMITH, G., A Dynamic IS-LM Simulation Model, in: Applied Economics 12, 1980, 313 - 327

SMITH, G., Flexible Policies and IS-LM Dynamics, in: Journal of Macroeconomics 4, 1982, 155 - 178

SMITH, G., The Long-Run Consequences of Monetary and Fiscal Policies when the Government Budget is Not Balanced, in: Journal of Public Economics 11, 1979, 59 - 79

SMITH, G., Monetarism, Bondism, and Inflation, in: Journal of Money, Credit and Banking 14, 1982, 278 - 286

SMYTH, D. J., Built-in-Flexibility of Taxation, the Government Budget Constraint, the Specification of the Demand for Money Function and the Stability of an IS-LM System, in: Public Finance 33, 1978, 367 - 375

SOLOW, R. M., Is There a Core of Usable Macroeconomics We Should All Believe in?, in: American Economic Review, Papers and Proceedings 87, 1997, 230 - 232

SOLOW, R. M., Models of Economic Growth, in: J. B. Taylor, M. Woodford, Eds., Handbook of Macroeconomics, Amsterdam (forthcoming)

SPAVENTA, L., The Growth of Public Debt: Sustainability, Fiscal Rules, and Monetary Rules, in: IMF Staff Papers 34, 1987, 374 - 399

STEIN, J. L., Ed., Monetarism, Amsterdam 1976

STEIN, J. L., Monetarist, Keynesian and New Classical Economics, New York 1982

TAYLOR, J. B., WOODFORD, M., Eds., Handbook of Macroeconomics, Amsterdam (forthcoming)

TOBIN, J., The Monetary-Fiscal Mix: Long-Run Implications, in: American Economic Association, Papers and Proceedings 76, 1986, 213 - 218

TOBIN, J., BUITER, W., Long-Run Effects of Fiscal and Monetary Policy on Aggregate Demand, in: J. L. Stein, Ed., Monetarism, Amsterdam 1976

TOBIN, J., DE MACEDO, J. B., The Short-Run Macroeconomics of Floating Exchange Rates: An Exposition, in: J. Chipman, C. Kindleberger, Eds., Flexible Exchange Rates and the Balance of Payments, New York 1981

TURNOVSKY, S. J., The Dynamics of an Open Economy with Endogenous Monetary and Fiscal Policies, in: Weltwirtschaftliches Archiv 115, 1979, 201 - 223

TURNOVSKY, S. J., The Dynamics of Fiscal Policy in an Open Economy, in: Journal of International Economics 6, 1976, 115 - 142

TURNOVSKY, S. J., Macroeconomic Analysis and Stabilization Policies, Cambridge 1977

TURNOVSKY, S. J., Methods of Macroeconomic Dynamics, Cambridge 1995

TURNOVSKY, S. J., Monetary and Fiscal Policy in a Long-Run Macroeconomic Model, in: Economic Record 56, 1980, 158 - 170

WANG, L. F. S., IS-LM Stability and Economic Policy Effectiveness: A Note, in: Journal of Macroeconomics 2, 1980, 175 - 179

WENZEL, H. D., Defizitfinanzierung als Instrument einer zielorientierten Finanzpolitik, Baden-Baden 1983

Printing: Druckhaus Beltz, Hemsbach
Binding: Buchbinderei Schäffer, Grünstadt